ommission Booklet

Conifers

Alan F. Mitchell
Forestry Commission

including a revision of some text originally written by
the late Herbert L. Edlin

LONDON: HER MAJESTY'S STATIONERY OFFICE

© Crown copyright 1985
First published 1966
Third edition 1985

ISBN 0 11 710040 4

ODC 174.7:(033):(410)

HER MAJESTY'S STATIONERY OFFICE

Government Bookshops

49 High Holborn, London WC1V 6HB
13a Castle Street, Edinburgh EH2 3AR
Brazennose Street, Manchester M60 8AS
Southey House, Wine Street, Bristol BS1 2BQ
258 Broad Street, Birmingham B1 2HE
80 Chichester Street, Belfast BT1 4JY

*Government publications are also available
through booksellers*

Acknowledgements

Key drawings by Marc Sale and John Williams.

Line drawings (for species included in the original edition) by David Walker.

Line drawings (for species added in this revised edition) by John Williams.

Figures 11 and 43 are taken from Forestry Commission Booklet 33 *Conifers in the British Isles* and were drawn by Christine Darter.

Colour photographs from the Forestry Commission collection, or by Maurice Nimmo where indicated.

Contents

Introduction

Conifers, or softwood trees, form a distinct group which has become very important in the world's economy because they grow fast on poor soils even under harsh climates, and yield timbers that are very suitable for industry. By comparison with the broadleaved trees or hardwoods, the conifers have a simple structure and pattern of growth. They are now being planted and tended on an increasing scale in most countries as a source of wealth, and this booklet shows how to identify those commonly found in British woods and parks.

First of all, make sure that the tree is in fact a conifer, and not some unusual broadleaved tree. Distinctive characters of the conifers include:

(a) Narrow, needle-like or scale-like leaves.
(b) Foliage usually evergreen (the only common exception being the larches).
(c) Scaly buds.
(d) Regular, almost geometrical, branching habit.
(e) Resinous fragrance of foliage, buds, bark and timber.
(f) Male and female flowers always borne separately, though usually on the same tree.
(g) Flowers always wind-pollinated, and therefore catkin-like, lacking showy petals or nectar.
(h) Fruit in the form of a woody cone (rarely, as in yew and juniper, a fleshy berry).
(i) Seeds usually winged.
(j) Seedlings of most kinds have numerous seed-leaves or cotyledons.

Only one common broadleaved tree, the alder, has a fruit-body at all like a cone. But the alder is a deciduous tree with an irregular branching habit and curious stalked buds, so at no season of the year can it be mistaken for a conifer.

Botanically, the conifers are classed as Gymnosperms, or 'naked seeded' plants, because their ovules, which later become seeds, are born exposed on the scales of the immature cones or female flowers. These ovules are fertilised, as with other plants, by pollen carried from male flowers. As the cones develop, their scales become tightly shut to protect the seeds within. But when once they are ripe the cone-scales open in dry weather, and then the winged seeds drift away. Most conifers flower in spring; their cones may ripen during the following autumn, the following spring, or in some species 18 months after pollination.

If the seeds alight on suitable ground, and are not eaten by squirrels, mice, birds, or insects, they germinate and produce a little whorl of seed-leaves, only two or three for some species but numerous in others. These are followed by an upright shoot that bears solitary needles, forming 'juvenile' foliage. Such solitary needles are found at the tops or tips of most sorts of conifers, and as they all look much alike they give little help towards identification. But the shoots formed in the seedling's *second* year, and on side or secondary branches in the foliage generally, have an 'adult' pattern of leaves. This is very distinctive for each genus of tree, and the following section shows how the genera can be sorted out with its aid.

In natural forests throughout the temperate zones of the world, and on mountain ranges in the tropics, conifers grow readily from seed, unaided by man. In cultivation they are raised in nurseries, nearly always from seed, since most kinds are very hard to grow from cuttings. So the sketches mostly illustrate two important nursery stages – the one-year-old *seedling* and the *transplant*, a tree that has been grown to a larger size after moving (lining out) into a transplant bed. One object of these sketches is to show foresters a good type of seedling raised in one year, and a suitable young transplant, two or three years old in all, for planting out in the forest.

The timber of conifers is always called *softwood*, though in a few species it is quite hard. On the whole, however, it is softer and easier to work than the *hardwood* yielded by broadleaved trees. This explains its much greater demand and value for most everyday uses, even though selected hardwoods, in small quantities suited to special purposes such as furniture-making, may fetch higher prices. Today the great bulk of timber used in house building, fencing, packing cases and boxes of all kinds, and as railway sleepers, telegraph poles, pitprops, is softwood. For paper-making, which uses about half of the output of wood in the main timber-growing countries, softwood is more suitable than hardwood because, amongst other features, its fibres are substantially longer. Softwood is also very suitable for the manufacture of most kinds of artificial board, an expanding industry that gives us wood chipboard, hardboard, and insulation board. At the present time about nine-tenths of all timber used in Britain, whether in the unaltered state or made up into paper or manufactured board, comes from coniferous trees.

We have only three native conifers, the Scots pine, the yew, and the juniper, and only the first of these ranks as a timber-yielding tree. Foresters have therefore brought in a large number of other kinds from Europe, North and South America, and the temperate parts of Asia. Many of these are grown only for ornament and in parks and gardens. Repeated trials over the past 100 years have shown that about a dozen of these *exotic* or introduced conifers are very suitable for timber production in the British Isles, and these kinds are now planted on a large scale. These 12 and the three native kinds, are featured here, together with a few of the most widespread and common park and garden trees. These conifers belong to five botanical families. The first helpful stage in classifying them is their genus, and the 38 kinds described here fall in 20 genera. Each genus has quite distinct features, and all can be told apart by foliage alone.

But do not rely on a single feature when naming trees. Look at the pictures and the main text before reaching a decision. Often some simple but unmistakable detail, such as the straight three-pointed bracts found on the cones of Douglas fir, will clear up all doubts very quickly.

The next subdivision of trees is the species, which is shown by the second word in each scientific name, for example, the European larch is *Larix decidua*, while the Japanese larch is *Larix kaempferi*, though both belong to the same genus, *Larix*, the larches.

The differences between species are relatively small, and call for close observation of form and colour, as explained in the general text. But these small differences are very important to the forester, because one species may thrive where a very similar one fails. For example, Sitka spruce grows well under exposure to salt winds along the west coast, but Norway spruce will not survive there. Nowadays foresters often study even finer differences within a single species, such as the *provenance*, or original homeland of a particular strain, but these precise distinctions are seldom obvious to the eye, and they are not dealt with here.

The aberrant forms of species, common in gardens but not planted in forests, are called 'cultivars' and are given a third name, e.g. *Taxus baccata* 'Fastigiata'. The third name is written in Roman type, not italics, and is placed in single quotes.

Because several botanists may have given Latin names and descriptions to the same tree at different times, and only one such name is now accepted, it is necessary to add, in the full citation of each specific name, the name or initials of the 'authority' for it. For example the Scots pine is called *Pinus sylvestris* L. , after the great Swedish botanist Linnaeus, who first called it that and published a full botanical description of it.

All this may sound complex at first, but with a specimen of the tree before you, and these pictures and text as a guide, it should soon be possible to name most conifers planted on a large scale. Descriptions of rarer kinds must be sought in larger textbooks but it is worth noting that most of them, too, belong to genera whose foliage features are described below.

Footnote for foresters

Our sketches of one-year *seedlings* illustrate the amount of shoot and root growth that a good nurseryman should expect to get in one season.

Even more important, our sketches of *transplants* show, for each kind of tree, the desirable size, sturdiness, and balance of shoot and root growth that are most likely to prove successful for forest planting.

A full description of all conifers commonly grown in Britain will be found in Forestry Commission Booklet No. 33, entitled *Conifers in the British Isles*, by A. F. Mitchell. This was published in 1972 by Her Majesty's Stationery Office (now priced £3.40). It includes 203 drawings and 24 photographs.

Key drawings

Botanists have classified the conifers by *genera* which are, fortunately, very useful to foresters who wish to name any kind. For example, all the spruces belong to a genus with the Latin name of *Picea*. All our commonly grown genera show quite distinctive leaf, or needle, arrangements on their normal, or 'adult', side branches. So, to discover the genus to which any conifer belongs, examine a side branch carefully, ignoring the youngest bit nearest to its tip.

But note that certain characteristic leaf patterns *cannot* be found on the upright leading shoots, nor on young seedlings, nor on many of the ornamental strains grown in gardens. Such branches often bear 'juvenile' foliage with a different pattern.

Having selected a side branch, note whether the leaves are set in open arrangement, so that you can clearly see the twig that bears them, or whether they hug the twig so closely that neither it

nor the buds can be seen. If the leaves are hard, leathery, spined and incurved 2.3cm long, the tree is a **Monkey puzzle**, *Araucaria*. If the foliage as a whole resembles the flattish fronds of a fern, the tree probably belongs to the Cypress family which includes **Lawson cypress**, and *Thuja*, **Western red cedar.** If not fern-like but open and branching it may be a **true cypress**, *Cupressus*. If the scale leaves have hard, rising points and are set on cord-like shoots it may be **Giant sequoia**, *Sequoiadendron*.

Many other common conifers have needles which stand clear of the twigs. In the genus *Larix*, the **larches**, they are set in clusters of 20–30, all springing from a little round woody knob, technically a 'short-shoot'. As the larches are deciduous and lose their leaves in winter, all you can find at that time of the year will be the woody knobs, but these too are quite distinctive. Bigger woody knobs with wrinkled tops show it is *Ginkgo*. *Cedrus*, the **cedars**, have

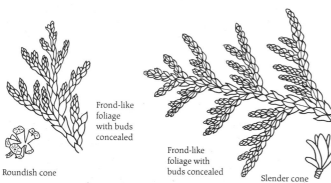

Frond-like foliage with buds concealed

Roundish cone

Fern-like foliage with buds and twigs hidden; roundish cone: Lawson cypress *Chamaecyparis lawsoniana*, pp. 20–21.

Frond-like foliage with buds concealed

Slender cone

Fern-like foliage with buds and twigs hidden; slender cone: Western red cedar *Thuja plicata*, pp. 60–61.

Leathery deciduous leaves with fan-veining: Maidenhair tree *Ginkgo biloba*, p. 27.

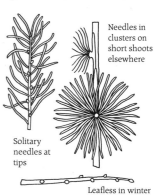

Needles in clusters on short shoots elsewhere

Solitary needles at tips

Leafless in winter

Most needles in clusters on woody knobs; solitary needles at twig tips: Larch *Larix* spp., pp. 30–33.

Spirally set leaves on new shoot. Whorls of leaves on spurs on 2-year wood: Cedar *Cedrus* spp., pp. 17–19.

the same arrangement but with hard, spined evergreen needles. The remaining conifers have their needles in groups of two or three, or else set singly. The **junipers** of the genus *Juniperus* bear sharp-pointed needles in groups of three, set all round the stem. The common form is a small shrub with a resinous scent.

Next, the **pines** of the genus *Pinus*, which are very commonly planted. These have their needles grouped in twos, threes or fives.

Needles in pairs (as here), threes, or fives, with a sheath at the base: Pine *Pinus* spp., pp. 42–50.

The three commonest kinds have their needles in *twos*, that is in pairs that spring from a basal sheath. See pages 42 to 46 and 48 to 49. One has them in threes and one has them in fives.

This leaves a group of conifers with isolated needles set singly. On most of these, the needles on side shoots appear to form two ranks, though they actually arise all around the twigs.

One genus is easily known because the needles are very variable in length, shorter ones being interspersed with longer ones. This is the **hemlock,** or *Tsuga* genus, described on pages 62 to 63.

Another genus, *Taxus*, the **yews**, can be told by green twigs and minute leafy buds at the tips of twigs (pages 58 to 59).

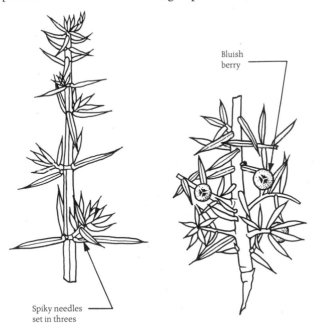

Bluish berry

Spiky needles set in threes

Needles in threes, all round stem, blue berries: Juniper *Juniperus* spp., pp. 28–29.

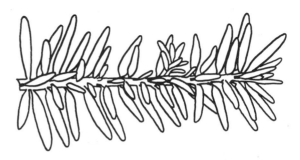

Solitary needles, irregular in length: Hemlock *Tsuga* spp., pp. 62–63.

Three common genera need rather more examination. Look closely at the foot of each needle to see whether it is springing directly from the flat surface of the twig, or whether it stands upon a little woody peg. If a peg is present, then the tree is a **spruce**, of the genus *Picea*. Check this by gently pulling a needle away; the peg will be drawn away also, leaving an irregular scar when it breaks off. Look further down the twig, to the point where older needles have *fallen* away; you will see that when the needles fall *naturally*, the pegs are always left behind, standing out like tiny hat-pegs. See pages 36 to 41.

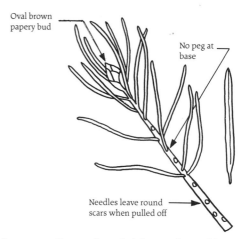

Needle, with minute stalk, rises from slightly raised, round base; papery pointed bud: Douglas fir *Pseudotsuga* spp., pp. 51–52.

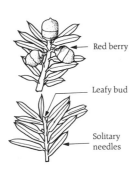

Minute leafy bud; red berries: Yew *Taxus* spp., pp. 58–59.

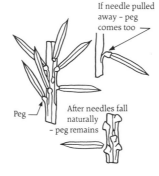

Needles on pegs: Spruce *Picea* spp., pp. 36–41.

If no pegs can be seen, then check as before by pulling away a needle. If it leaves a small round scar, then the tree is either a **Silver fir** of the genus *Abies* or else a **Douglas fir** of the genus *Pseudotsuga*. Check by looking at an older twig from which needles have fallen, and you will find that its surface is smooth, without projections.

The Douglas fir can easily be told apart from the commonly grown Silver firs by its slender, brown papery buds, and minute stalks at needle bases. The buds of the Silver firs are blunter, and often resinous. The Douglas fir is described on pages 51 to 52, and the Silver firs on pages 10 to 14.

Needle arising from a flat, round base; blunt bud: Silver fir *Abies* spp., pp. 10–14.

Two more genera can be distinguished by their thin, fragile fresh green leaves which are deciduous in autumn. If the leaves are very slender and alternate on shoots which are alternate it is *Taxodium*, **Swamp cypress**. If the leaves are broad oblongs, oppositely set on oppositely placed shoots, it is *Metasequoia*, **Dawn redwood**.

If the leaves are hard and dark, evergreen like yew but banded white beneath, the green shoot will have long scales with free tips and the tree is *Sequoia*, **Coast redwood**.

All parts in opposite pairs; leaves and side shoots deciduous: Dawn redwood *Metasequoia glyptostroboides*, pp. 34–35.

Leaves and shoots spirally or alternately held, both deciduous: Swamp cypress *Taxodium* spp., p. 57.

Scale leaves on shoot; linear, flat hard leaves on laterals: Coast redwood *Sequoia sempervirens*, pp. 53–54.

Abies grandis

The Silver firs which make up the genus *Abies* are known by their needles, which are always solitary, usually leathery, and which leave a neat round scar on the twig when they are pulled away. A glance at the buds will distinguish them from two rather similar conifers; in the Douglas fir the buds are slender with brown papery scales, while in the yew the buds are small, with leafy scales free at the tips. No common Silver fir has buds quite like those; Silver fir buds are short, plump, and often resinous.

Silver firs always form erect stems and show a regular branching pattern. For many years their bark remains smooth, except for resin blisters, though old trees show shallow plates or fissures. The male flowers are like those of many other conifers, being simply clusters of yellow stamens, but the female flowers and cones are distinctive (see page 14). The female flower, an upright, green, oval structure which opens near the tips of side branches in May, expands rapidly during the summer, and is ripe by late August. Unlike other common cones, it remains upright, but only remains intact for a few weeks. Each scale has a bract below it, and once the cone turns brown both bract and scale break away and fall, releasing a pair of winged seeds. The central spike or axis of the cone remains standing for a year or so; it is called the 'fir candle' and is a sure recognition sign. Anyone who needs Silver fir seed must be quick off the mark, and collect his cones by climbing the tree as soon as they are ripe. Also intact cones are hard to store as specimens, even if held together by wires.

Silver fir seeds are rather large, and have a triangular wing firmly attached to both sides of the seed. They are hard to store, and in practice are sown in the spring after they ripen. The seedlings have few seed-leaves, three to six or so (Figures 1 and 2), followed by normal foliage. They start growth slowly and are usually kept for 2 years in the seedbed; after transplanting they take another 2 years to reach the plantable size illustrated here.

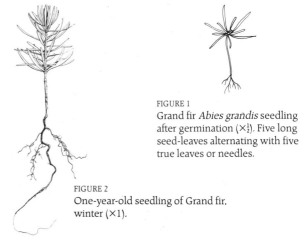

FIGURE 1
Grand fir *Abies grandis* seedling after germination (×⅓). Five long seed-leaves alternating with five true leaves or needles.

FIGURE 2
One-year-old seedling of Grand fir, winter (×1).

The European Silver fir, *Abies alba* Miller, flourishes on the Pyrenees, Vosges, the Jura, the Alps and many other mountain ranges. During the 19th century this species was widely planted in the British Isles and some fine specimen trees still survive. Unfortunately, about the year 1900, the aphid *Adelges nordmannianae* (Ekstein), which had been accidentally introduced from eastern Europe, began to damage the younger trees growing in Britain; it has proved so serious in our milder climate that the European species is no longer planted for timber. Rugged old specimens remain common only in parts of Scotland, especially Argyll and Perthshire and in southern Ireland. Some are around 45m × 5.5m. The grey, sparsely hairy shoot bears very dark green leaves spread each side of the shoot, and dull brown, globose, non-resinous buds. The bark is dark grey in shallow small plates; paler, almost silvery on young trees and high in the crown.

FIGURE 3
Grand fir transplant, aged 3 years (2+1); the buds are blunt, winter (×¼).

FIGURE 4
Spray of Grand fir foliage, with needles flatly disposed in two ranks (×¼).

In its place foresters use the Grand fir from western North America, which is shown here. Though it resembles the European kind, it suffers no serious harm from insect pests. Its needles lie in very flat planes, and are somewhat variable in length; its buds are resinous, a feature that distinguishes it from the European sort. Because it stands shade when young, it is often planted below birch, larch, or other trees giving only a light overhead cover. A good crop of Grand fir yields a great volume of timber in a relatively short time, and for this reason this tree is now being planted on a growing, though still small, scale.

The timber of the Silver firs is very like that of the spruces (page 41); in fact it is sometimes imported from Europe under the same trade name of 'whitewood'. It is pale cream or brown in colour, without apparent heartwood, and is suitable for joinery, house-building, box-making, and paper pulp; though not naturally durable out of doors, it is readily treated with preservatives.

Growth of Grand fir is very rapid and, in damp, sheltered glens, sustained. Many are now, when quite young, 50–55m tall and one, planted in 1875 near Loch Fyne in Argyll (Strone House), is equal tallest tree in Britain (1982) at 60m.

CAUCASIAN FIR

Abies nordmanniana

Replacing the Common silver fir in most large gardens, the Caucasian fir has been grown here since 1848 and is now reasonably common. Except in the north and west of Scotland, it does not seem likely to achieve the sizes that were common in the silver fir and in the south-east the oldest are dying at the top when only 40m tall. Despite that, the young trees are vigorous, handsome and usually healthy, with foliage of great luxuriance on some trees. This differs from the foliage of Common silver fir in the leaves being longer and harder and lying right across the top of the shoot, not parted. The bark is similarly grey in small blocks but the crown is more regularly conic and not as broad or as heavily branched.

FIGURE 5
Caucasian fir *Abies nordmanniana*. Trees vary strongly from this rather open foliage to densely luxuriant with upstanding leaves hiding the shoot ($\times\frac{2}{3}$).

NOBLE FIR

Abies procera

This handsome conifer, which formerly bore the scientific name of *A. nobilis* Lindley, is readily known by the upswept form of the needles on its side twigs. These needles are a bluish-grey in colour, and the whole tree is remarkably decorative; in Denmark it is preferred to all other conifers as a Christmas tree. Its native home is North America where it grows to great size in the forests of Washington and Oregon. The growth habit is remarkably regular, but the trunk tends to taper more markedly than do most other trees; the bark is pale grey to purplish.

Noble fir cones are remarkable for their large bracts, which are bent downwards and give each cone a feathery outline; in America it is sometimes called 'feathercone fir' (Figure 10). In the west of Scotland the Noble fir has shown good resistance to gales off the sea, and also to harsh winters, and as it can give high yields of timber it is now being planted on a small scale in western districts generally. It is most likely to be found, however, as an ornamental tree many of which, in Scotland, are 40–45m tall, 1.5m diameter. The timber resembles that of other Silver firs.

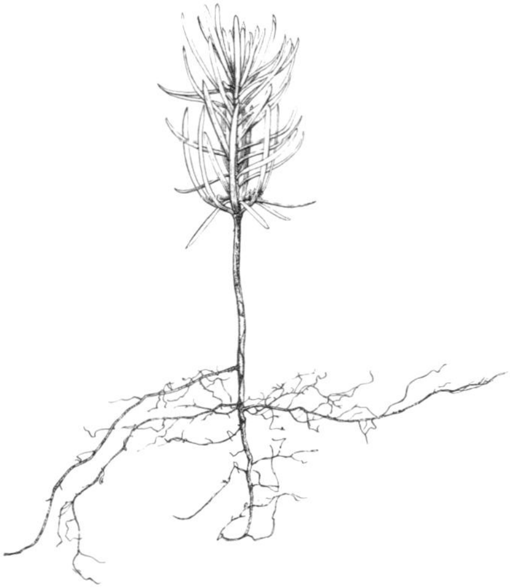

FIGURE 6
One-year-old seedling of Noble fir *Abies procera*, winter (×¾).

FIGURE 7
Transplant of Noble fir aged 3 years (2+1); foliage is upswept, winter (×¼).

FIGURE 8
(below top): Female flower (centre) and foliage of Noble fir, spring (×¼).

FIGURE 9
(below bottom): Male flowers (centre) and foliage of Noble fir, spring (×¼).

FIGURE 10
(below): 'Feathercone' of Noble fir; note reflexed bracts and also the upswept foliage, September (×⅓).

Araucaria araucana

The first trees of this now common, if peculiar tree, were raised in 1795 by Archibald Menzies on board ship on his journey from Chile, where he took the nuts from a banquet table, to Kew. A few trees were raised around 1825–35 but the first big import of seed, from which great numbers of our biggest trees were raised arrived in 1843. In general, the best specimens are in western areas from Devon through north Wales to Argyll but there are some big trees in eastern and midland areas although they are usually less thriving. It became fashionable around 1850–60 to plant this tree in town and suburban gardens, which do not suit it at all well and the thin unhappy trees commonly resulting have given the tree a bad name but a thriving specimen is remarkably handsome.

The Monkey puzzle family is scattered across the southern hemisphere and is a primitive group. The species we grow has separate male and female trees, and although some individual pairs differ markedly in shape of crown, taken as a whole, no differences in growth can be found between the sexes. Many are reluctant to flower, but until they do it cannot be known whether they are male or female. Male flowering trees bear three or four long sausage-shaped flowers at the ends of many shoots. The pollen is shed in quantity in late June and the flowers often adhere, dark brown until the winter. Female trees are known by large, globular spiny cones, bright green with yellow-tipped spines in their second year and darker, then falling to pieces as they shed seed towards the end of the third year. The seed will be empty unless there is a male tree within about 100 metres, and there will be 200 seeds in a full cone.

The seed germinates in an unusual manner, the cotyledons and seed staying below the ground and a small shoot emerging with spirally set broad needles. Seed from a tree close to a male should yield about 95 per cent germination. Early growth is slow and for several years the tree is scorched by hard frosts but normally without damaging effect. The whorls of branches do not necessarily reflect one year's growth as they do in many other conifers. Sometimes they are the growth of a single year but more often two whorls take 3 years to grow, or there is only one in each 2 years. Growth in height is rarely more than 40cm for some years, then it is less, and no tree is currently known more than 30m tall. They should be planted only when less than 45cm tall, with the roots carefully spread, and kept clean of weeds and especially tall grass for 5 years.

The timber is seldom available and is very resinous in home-grown trees but has been made into interior shelving. In Argentina they were used in vast quantities for railway sleepers, but none is cut now. It is similar to the Parana pine, *Araucaria angustifolia*, which is commonly imported.

FIGURE 11
Mature shoot of Chile pine or Monkey puzzle *Araucaria araucana* showing the closely spaced spine-tipped leaves (×½).

INCENSE CEDAR

Calocedrus decurrens

This is one of many trees of the Cypress family which grow in the south-western United States in an open, level-branched form but in England, especially in the east, grow immediately into strictly upright-branched, dense columns. As a neat, narrow columnar tree this is valuable in landscaping and for confined spaces although it grows steadily, but not very fast, to 35m. It is reasonably common in parks and gardens but is not good in towns.

The bright green scale leaves are in opposite pairs, one pair having an extended base clothing the shoot, unlike those of any other cypress-like tree. Handling the foliage causes a strong turpentine scent, like some shoe-polishes, to be emitted. Male flowers are dense in some years and on some trees, bright yellow at the tips of the shoots. Female flowers on the same tree ripen into small, leathery flask-shaped cones soon conspicuously yellow. The seed yielded by any tree in a group is likely to be very fertile and seedlings, at first with spreading needle-scales, grow quickly into slender-crowned upright trees. The bark is deep red-brown, coarsely fissured into big plates running vertically for several metres.

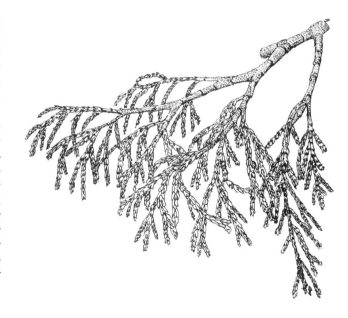

FIGURE 12
Foliage of Incense cedar *Calocedrus decurrens* ($\times \frac{2}{3}$). Each scale leaf has an extended rectangular basal part unlike any similar foliage in the cypresses and thujas.

Cedrus atlantica

The normal wild form of this tree was sent in 1841 from Algeria and is rather uncommon. It is a deep green rather broadly crowned, strongly branched tree seen in churchyards and some gardens. In 1845, a form with blue-grey foliage was found in one valley and brought to England. Its various seedling selections, var. *glauca*, have been very commonly planted for a long time. The Blue Atlas cedar grows very rapidly (unless it is planted when 2–3m tall, when it will grow very slowly for many years) on almost any well-drained soil, including chalk, and is highly tolerant of drought and, to some extent tolerant of exposure and of impure air. It is therefore a valuable tree in garden design in and around

towns. It soon becomes much too big for its place as a centre plant in a rose-garden or small lawn, where it is too frequently seen planted. The crown is fairly regularly broad-conic with age, narrower at first, and the bark, sometimes brown, is more often pale grey and finely divided into shallow, raised rectangular plates. The colour varies with the stock from which the graft was taken, or with seedling origin, but is paler blue-grey than any other cedar, and in some selections, bright white. The needles are shorter than those of Lebanon cedars, 2cm or less, and the flowers open earlier, in September. Self-sown seedlings grow up in one or two gardens so the seed may often be fertile.

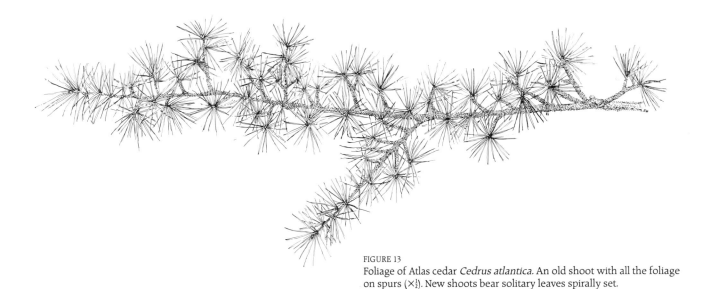

FIGURE 13
Foliage of Atlas cedar *Cedrus atlantica.* An old shoot with all the foliage on spurs (×½). New shoots bear solitary leaves spirally set.

DEODAR

Cedrus deodara

Sent from the Punjab first in 1831, the deodar was soon very commonly planted as a screen around houses which were then on the outskirts of towns and are now in suburbia, in large gardens and in churchyards, cemeteries and parks. It survives moderately impure town air quite well but makes a bigger, more heavily foliaged tree in country areas, where many are 30m tall and 1.3m through the bole. Young trees are very pendulous and tend to have grey foliage for some years before turning deep green. Old trees retain their shapely form and drooping tip, although some have forked or have big, upturned branches. They differ from the Lebanon cedar in this narrow, conic crown, retained to the tip; in the drooped leading shoot and shoots at the outside of the crown; in the longer needles, 6cm against 4cm; and in an ashen grey colour on the ridges of the bark. The flowers and cones are very similar, although the cones are taller.

FIGURE 15
Cedrus cone (×½). The three common true cedars bear cones distinguishable only by minor features.

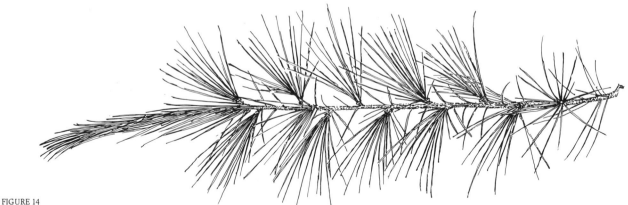

FIGURE 14
Deodar cedar *Cedrus deodara.* Spirally set solitary leaves on the new shoot (×½); whorled leaves on spurs on old wood, as in all true cedars and larches.

18

Cedrus libani

The true cedars, quite distinct from the many cypresses, junipers and redwoods often called 'cedar', are an Old World group of only four species. Three grow in the Mediterranean region and one in the western Himalayas. Three of the four are very common trees, the fourth, from Cyprus, is very rare.

The first cedar grown here was the Cedar of Lebanon which was first raised in 1640. The hard winter of 1740 killed nearly all the early trees and most of the huge and seemingly ancient cedars on mansion lawns date in fact from the big plantings made from 1760 to 1820. After some years as a slender, spire-like tree, this cedar grows very fast indeed and soon becomes a big tree with heavy, spreading branches. Many of the old trees have exten-sive, flat tops 25–30m tall but a few grow taller, above 35m, and one in a wood is a narrow tree 46m tall.

The slender, hard, sharply pointed needles are spirally set singly, around new shoots but in whorls of 40–50 on spurs along older shoots. The female flower grows in the centre of a whorl, pale pink or bright green and only 3mm or so across, and takes a year to mature into a 12cm, tall cylindric blue-green cone, which becomes woody and dark brown during the next year. The flower opens in October, the cedars being our only autumn-flowering conifers. Male flowers stand erect above the flat array of foliage, green and blue-grey during the summer, yellow with pollen as they lengthen in October, then they curve over at the tip and fall off. October is not a good season here for pollen to dry and ripen or to be blown on dry winds, so the seed is frequently empty.

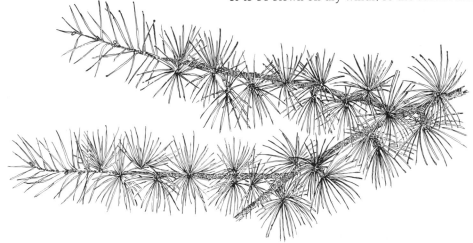

FIGURE 16
Cedar of Lebanon *Cedrus libani* foliage (×⅓). In length of needle, half way between the Algerian cedar and the Deodar.

Chamaecyparis lawsoniana

The natural range of this tree is very limited, being a short stretch of coast from Oregon to California, and the hills behind, with one small detached area further inland. It was first sent in 1854 and has long been the commonest of all decorative conifers in Britain and the backbone and mainstay of every large garden. This is partly due to its tolerance of almost any soil, its ease of propagation by both seed and cuttings and its reliable growth everywhere, but even more from the huge variety of forms and colours. The second seed-lot in 1855 gave one bright green, very erect form, 'Erecta Viridis' and although remarkably uniform in America, there has been a constant stream of new colour and foliage forms from this tree ever since in British and Dutch nurseries.

The male flowers are abundant every year, pinkish purple to dark red, at the tips of the smallest shoots. Behind them are the numerous females, powder-blue, ripening to globose grey-white

FIGURE 18

Silhouettes of Lawson cypress varieties. Left to right: 'Allumii' With age this bushes out around the base. 'Erecta' Very liable to have branches bent out by wet snow. 'Lutea' The first bright golden form raised, and still not surpassed.

FIGURE 17

Lawson cypress *Chamaecyparis lawsoniana* seedling showing shoot of adult foliage arising from juvenile leaves (×1).

cones which soon become woody and brown and shed great quantities of seed. A few small finches and tits are starting to feed on these but the great attraction of this tree for birds is its provision of early spring shelter for nests of thrushes, blackbirds, dunnocks, chaffinches, greenfinches and others, and the high cover for all the year for many other birds. The seeds germinate easily and the seedlings raised grow fast, but there is a great mixture of shades of green, from yellowish through grey to bluish, in the resulting plants. The named cultivars are raised from cuttings, which are somewhat slow to root and slow in early growth.

20

The most notable cultivars commonly planted are:

'Allumii'
Narrowly conic from a bushy base, dark blue-grey interior, light blue-grey new foliage. The most commonly seen form in suburban gardens.

'Erecta Viridis'
Flame-shaped, branchy, untidy where branches bent by snow, this is bright dark green and all too common in cemeteries and in gardens. It can achieve 30m in height.

'Lutea'
The oldest, and still as good as any, of the numerous bright golden forms. A narrow columnar crown has small branches with pendulous shoots and smooth warm brown bark scaling with age.

'Stewartii'
More broadly conic than 'Lutea', with stronger branching, this golden form has very distinct foliage with long flattened sprays of fern-like aspect and the side-shoots depressed. It has so far attained 20m.

'Triumph of Boskoop'
This is more vigorous than ordinary green Lawson cypress and grows into a better shape, usually a single strong stem to the top, in a tall, conic rather open crown. The light branches bear broad sprays of foliage which is at first bright blue-grey, later dark green.

'Wisselii'
The most extreme of the foliage forms, has a narrowly columnar crown with short branches turned up at the ends forming little spired turrets of congested, twisted deep blue foliage with silvery white bands. It bears large quantities of rich deep red male flowers. It grows much faster than the appearance suggests and some trees 70 years old are 25m tall with boles over 1m through.

FIGURE 19
Foliage spray of Lawson cypress showing globular cones after opening, autumn ($\times\frac{1}{2}$).

Chamaecyparis nootkatensis

This tree inhabits cold damp slopes just below glaciers from Alaska to northern Oregon and is exceedingly hardy. Its use in cold, exposed places is limited, however, by a tendency not to be firm against gales from unexpected quarters. The crown is so uniformly conic that the tree is instantly recognisable from a great distance. This is so even when the main stem forks low down but whether the conic shape is narrow or broad depends very much on where the tree grows. In eastern England this is a slender tree particularly when young but in the west and more so in Ireland it is very soon broad and the conic crown of old trees is obtuse, and very often the base is surrounded by either layered branches or a ring of stout branches arising below 1m from the ground. Growth is quite rapid in young trees, but decidedly slow in old ones. Introduced by Jeffrey in 1851 in a very small quantity, few trees were planted until Lobb sent large amounts of seed in 1853. Trees of this age are found on many Scottish estates and are now over 27m tall but only one younger tree has been found over 30.5m.

The foliage hangs, dark and heavy, and when crushed gives a scent of turpentine. Variably pendulous, even those with the most pendent shoots are distinct from the Weeping Nootka, 'Pendula', in which the branches curve upwards and the foliage hangs in flat plates. The scales end in fine rigid points which make it difficult to rub the wrong way. The cones have a beak on each scale, a feature which is inherited in all the × *Cupressocyparis* hybrids of which this is a parent.

In landscaping, this tree is too dark and lifeless in foliage for use as other than an isolated specimen or as a close group where the regular conic crowns can make a good feature. Near and in towns the few trees seen are thin, gaunt and unattractive.

FIGURE 20
Nootka cypress *Chamaecyparis nootkatensis*. Harsh, hard, dark foliage in flattened sprays (×½).

SAWARA CYPRESS

Chamaecyparis pisifera

This Japanese species is uncommon except in gardens specializing in conifers which were planted soon after this tree was introduced in 1861, and in which this was among the normal complement of species then fashionable. These trees are often rather thin and dark in foliage, which is crowded with the pea-like cones from which the specific adjective is derived. Young trees, not often seen, are bright yellow-green and well furnished. Generally passed over as a form perhaps of Lawson cypress, the type tree with its very small, acutely pointed scales marked bright blue-white beneath is not well known. Several of its cultivars, however, raised in Japan and imported with it in 1861 are very common and familiar trees in urban parks, churchyards and gardens, but they are seldom identified and without handy common names they are ignored. 'Plumosa' and its golden form 'Plumosa Aurea' are very common, especially in churchyards and parks in towns and villages. They make dense, broadly columnar trees with several tops and can be over 20m tall. The bark is stringy and pale red-brown. Another, 'Squarrosa', known as the 'moss-cypress' in America, has no common name here but is fairly common. Its bark is a richer red and its fluffy foliage looks blue-grey from a short distance and is very soft to the touch. This form is less common in towns but is frequent in large gardens making a broadly conic tree sometimes to 25m in height. In all the forms of Sawara cypress the crushed foliage has an acrid resinous scent.

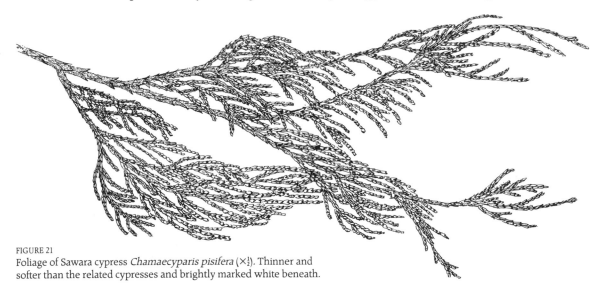

FIGURE 21
Foliage of Sawara cypress *Chamaecyparis pisifera* ($\times\frac{1}{2}$). Thinner and softer than the related cypresses and brightly marked white beneath.

× Cupressocyparis leylandii

This hybrid between the Nootka cypress and the Monterey cypress was first found as six plants raised from seed of a Nootka picked in 1888. The parent tree is at Leighton Hall, Powys. The second batch were picked from a Monterey cypress in 1911 at the same place. Subsequently others arose in Dorset (1940) and Northern Ireland (1962).

The Leyland most abundantly planted is derived from one of the 1888 trees, and is named 'Haggerston Grey' after the Northumberland estate on which the first six seedlings were planted. It has its foliage arising at all angles around the shoot, the finest branches much separated from each other and very dark green, slightly grey beneath. The next most commonly planted, 'Leighton Green' is from a 1911 tree growing at Leighton Hall and has thicker foliage, rich green, in flat, frond-like long shoots, the finest branchlets close together, more yellowish green beneath.

Leyland cypress is being planted in immense numbers in suburban and rural gardens and as screens for fruit-crops and general shelter. It has hybrid vigour in abundance and within 2–3 years is growing at 1m a year on almost any soil or site. There are only very few trees dating from before 1929 when it had been rediscovered 3 years and was propagated in numbers for the first time. Most of those now 45–50 years old are around 30 m tall and 70 cm in diameter and still growing fast.

The Haggerston trees rarely flower, but 'Leighton Green' flowers from an early age, with yellow males and 3cm cones on which each scale has a beak, inherited from the Nootka cypress. Both forms make upright-branched tall columnar crowns with a narrow apex. 'Leighton Green' tends to have bigger branches and to make a big bole more quickly. The form from Dorset, 'Stapehill 21' is scarcely distinguishable from 'Leighton Green'.

In 1962 two golden forms arose in Northern Ireland. 'Castle-wellan', now planted on a large scale, is a seedling of the golden Monterey cypress 'Lutea' and has foliage at all angles on the shoot and a tendency for the interior to be dark green, especially in winter, and the gold confined to the shoot tips. 'Robinson's Gold' was found as a seedling in Belvoir Park and has the flattened foliage of 'Leighton Green' but bright yellow, sometimes greening in winter. Other golden forms and some variegated with white are now being sold.

FIGURE 22
Foliage of Leyland cypress ×*Cupressocyparis leylandii* ($\times\frac{1}{4}$). Two varieties illustrated. Above: 'Haggerston Grey'. Slender final shoots widely parted; large spray at all angles. Below: 'Leighton Green'. Final shoots broad, often closely set; large spray much flattened.

Cupressus

The first cypress grown in Britain was the Italian cypress, *Cupressus sempervirens* L. which was here by 1550. No other cypress was known and this one was not then very hardy. During this century this has not been damaged by even the hardest winters but it is seldom planted and its slender dark conic form is seen in few gardens. It has dark foliage of small scale leaves and big rounded dull grey-brown cones, very like that of Monterey cypress but it is unlike that in its form and growth.

The Monterey cypress, *Cupressus macrocarpa* Hartw. grows wild only on a mile or so of low cliffs near Monterey, California. The first seed arrived mysteriously at Kew in 1838 but large quantities were sent in 1850 and it is now abundant in many parts of Britain. It is particularly so in Cornwall and south Devon as a shelter-tree and in towns, parks and gardens. It is a common park and garden tree through the Midlands to East Anglia and in the Weald but is uncommon in Scotland. In the south-west it rapidly grows into a hugely spreading tree with long, low branches and is often 1.5 to 2m through the bole in less than 100 years but rarely above 32m in height. In the Midlands and eastern England it is often a narrowly upright tree, and rarely so big. The foliage is rather fleshy, closely held scale leaves, bright green, dark on old trees and when crushed it gives a lemony scent. Male flowers are yellow, crowded at the tips of shoots of mature trees in some years, shedding pollen in June. The females are yellow and orange rosettes on older shoots, ripening to woody irregularly globular cones 4–5cm through.

Timber from the trees usually seen will be far too knotty to be of value, but a clean bole gives high quality strong wood, and a few plantations have been made but the tree is difficult to raise and to transplant so its rapid growth is rarely made use of commercially. It is valued, however, in plantings to give shelter from strong sea-winds. This tree will not make a good hedge for long, as the lower branches die and it becomes thin at the base. For hedges and inland shelter it has been replaced by Leyland cypress (see page 24).

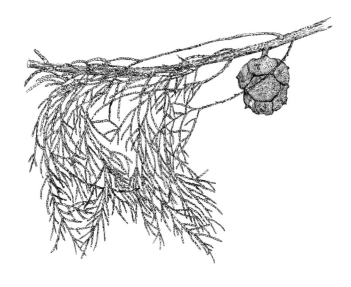

FIGURE 23
Foliage and cone of the Monterey cypress *Cupressus macrocarpa* ($\times\frac{1}{2}$). The cones develop from large yellow and orange flowers which open in June.

SMOOTH ARIZONA CYPRESS

Cupressus glabra

This soft, powder-blue, shapely tree is now quite common in suburban gardens and parks. It grows at a moderate rate on any well-drained soil, whether chalky or sandy and is never damaged by frost or by drought. The short-branched foliage at wide angles is lightly speckled with white spots of resin and when crushed gives a scent like grapefruit skin. The male flowers are light yellow and prominent from autumn through the winter until shedding pollen in May. The cones are bunched on thicker shoots, and are woody, purple-brown and stay on the tree for some years. Introduced in 1904 this tree was little planted until after 1950 and some of the few old trees are over 20m tall but still nearly conic. A bluer, more upright form 'Pyramidalis' has more resin-spots, one on nearly every scale leaf.

FIGURE 24
Foliage of the Smooth Arizona cypress *Cupressus glabra* (×½). Blue-grey, with white resin spots on a small proportion of the scale leaves.

FIGURE 25
Cone of the Smooth Arizona cypress (×½).

MAIDENHAIR TREE

Ginkgo biloba

The Ginkgo is in a botanical group of its own, more primitive than the conifers, and is the only plant of an entire Order to survive. The Ginkgo group were the dominant trees after the Coal Age and before conifers had evolved. It survived probably wild in tracts of forest in central China preserved from clearing because they were monastery woods. It was taken to Japan more than a thousand years ago and was discovered by the western world there in 1689. It was introduced to Holland in 1734 and to Britain in 1754. The original tree, moved to Kew in 1761 survives today.

The leaves emerge from flat disc-like dark brown buds in late April and are bright fresh green, darkening by early summer. In a sunny, hot, autumn, a Ginkgo in the open turns bright gold in late October. In winter the spiky bare crown is distinctive with the 1cm spurs which bear the leaves, projecting. Crown shape varies greatly, with some trees like poles with few branches and others with numerous big branches, spreading, twisting or upright, whilst most are somewhere between these extremes, tending to be slender with small, rising branches.

The trees are of separate sexes but male trees rarely flower until they are big and old, when slender catkins come out among the leaves. Female trees often flower when only 10m tall and, in Britain, they are nearly always shapely, slender trees, but they are quite scarce. The flower is like a small acorn on a long stalk and ripens into a fruit like a small plum, green thickly bloomed grey-blue. In autumn it turns pale pink-brown then darkens and falls. The fleshy husk then rots with a strong, unpleasant foetid smell.

Ginkgos are trees largely of southern towns. Many fine specimens are in and around London, Bath and Yeovil particularly and they tend to be in Cathedral closes and central parks. They are seen in East Anglia and to some extent in the Midlands but become rare in the west and north until in Scotland there are only small trees mostly south of Edinburgh but a few are further north on the eastern side, with one in Easter Ross.

Ginkgos are raised from seed imported from Italy or, more usually, the USA where it is a very common city and garden tree and where the long hot summers encourage them to flower and fruit heavily. Growth is erratic and can be 65cm one year and exactly 0 cm the next, the terminal bud opening only a rosette of leaves. This may occur 2 or 3 years in succession, then be followed by another 65cm shoot. Only small plants should be moved, up to 60cm, or establishment is difficult and slow. Good trees are growing on clays, gravels, sands and thin loam over chalk but it seems to prefer a soil base-rich or alkaline to a poor acid one and needs a somewhat damp site. Being quite unrelated to any other plant, and of ancient origin, Ginkgo remains pest-free as none of the modern pests is at home on it, but it is sometimes killed by Honey fungus.

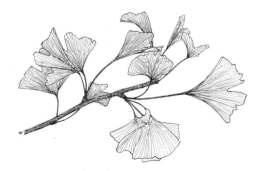

FIGURE 26
Foliage of the Maidenhair tree *Ginkgo biloba* (×¼). Thick and leathery, the leaves turn bright gold in a sunny autumn.

Juniperus chinensis

Chinese juniper is the usual Juniper of town parks and gardens and is often in churchyards. It is a dark, dull tree except when the male is thickly covered in yellow flowers through the winter. The crown is conic, broad at first and often remaining so in the lower parts, but may have a narrowly conic upper half. The bark is dull brown and stripping and the bole is mis-shapen, either with deep hollows or being two fused stems, and bears sprouts. The foliage is different from that of the Common juniper in that it is not all juvenile, projecting needles, but is mainly minute dark scale leaves clothing the stem, but mixed in the outer parts with small shoots of juvenile, stiff and prickly spreading needles.

The golden form 'Aurea' is common particularly in towns and is a more dense, columnar male tree arising in a Surrey nursery in 1855.

FIGURE 27
Chinese juniper *Juniperus chinensis* ($\times\frac{3}{4}$). The juvenile foliage is stiff and sharp; the adult is smooth.

COMMON JUNIPER

Juniperus communis

This is only a shrub, sometimes a miniature tree of 5–6m and is never planted in gardens but is included briefly as one of our three native conifers. It grows wild in two widely different environments. Small populations survive in a few places on fairly open scrubland on chalk downs in the south. Larger stands are found at 300m or more above sea-level in Cumbria and other northern hills on limestone and at lower level in a few valleys. But in the north of Scotland the tree is a small, straggly plant in the shade of old Scots pine woods on wet, peaty acid soils.

The needles are in whorls of three, sharp, dark blue-green, with white bands beneath and rather closely surrounding the shoot. The female flowers become fleshy, dark purple and very like a berry, but in its unripe, green stage it can be seen to be composed of several flat scales like the cones of a true cypress.

The Irish juniper, 'Hibernica' is quite common in small gardens or in rock or heather gardens. It is a very narrow, neat conic shape with dense, erect shoots, and is sometimes 5m tall but very slow in growth.

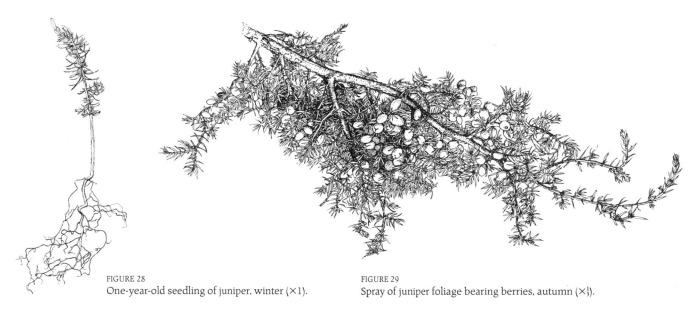

FIGURE 28
One-year-old seedling of juniper, winter (×1).

FIGURE 29
Spray of juniper foliage bearing berries, autumn (×⅓).

Larix decidua

Larches differ from other common conifers in being deciduous. Each spring they put forth fresh foliage, at first a bright emerald green but becoming duller later. Each autumn their needles fade to a pale straw colour then bright yellow and sometimes orange before they fall. But the needles on first year seedlings, and at the tips only of other very young trees, are often *evergreen*, as the pictures show.

On larches of all ages, the needles on first year shoots are always solitary. Everywhere else they grow in tufts or bunches, which are actually 'short shoots' that never grow longer. The presence of these little knobs makes the larches easy to identify, both in summer and also when they are leafless in winter. The male flowers, borne in spring as the delicate needles open, are clusters of golden anthers. The female flowers, often called 'larch roses', are pretty flower-like clusters of scales, and may be green, white, or deep pink in colour. They ripen within 6 months to rather cylindrical cones. These cones only slowly expand their scales, and to extract the seed they must be levered apart or opened by heat. The little seeds which eventually fall out and drift away are winged, the wing being firmly fixed to one side and lightly attached to the other.

The European larch, which is still the commonest kind though no longer that most frequently planted, can be told apart from other larches by its straw-coloured twigs, its true-green needles, and its straight cone-scales. It is native to the Alps and other mountain ranges of central Europe, and has been cultivated in Britain since the 17th century. Because strains or provenances from high Alpine ranges are not well suited to the British climate, foresters prefer to get their seed from the Sudeten mountains of Poland and Czechoslovakia, where strains exist that are known to do well in the British Isles.

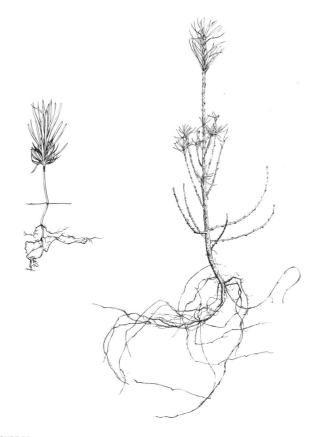

FIGURE 30
(left): One-year-old European larch *Larix decidua* seedling, winter. Note evergreen early needles ($\times\frac{1}{2}$).

FIGURE 31
European larch transplant aged 2 years (1+1) suitable for forest planting. Note evergreen needles on certain branch tips, although it is winter ($\times\frac{1}{3}$).

Larch timber has a pale creamy-brown sapwood and a distinctly reddish-brown, or terra cotta coloured, heartwood. This heartwood is naturally durable, and though nowadays most softwood – and also the sapwood of larch if necessary – can easily be treated to make them last just as long, this was formerly a great advantage. Larch timber as a whole has, moreover, better strength properties than most other conifers. For these reasons it is widely grown and used for fencing, gates, and estate repair work, and also in shipbuilding; the sturdy wooden fishing boats that are still built along the east coast of Scotland always have their outer planking made of a special grade of 'boat-skin' larch. Larch is a very adaptable tree which grows quickly in youth, but each tree needs ample light and space, and so the total timber crop is rather light. It has often been grown in mixture with broadleaved trees, to help 'nurse' or shelter them in their early stages. Sometimes a crop of larch is thinned out and *under-planted* with conifers of other kinds, which will take its place later on, and yield more timber; this is possible because larch casts only a light shade.

Because larch starts growth so quickly, it is usually planted out when only 2 years old; Figure 31 shows a '1 + 1' transplant. The bark on old trees is broken up by shallow cracks or fissures into long, coarsely scaly grey-brown ridges or plates.

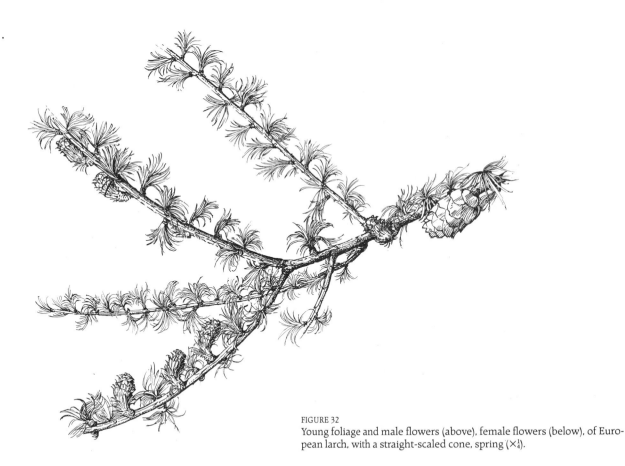

FIGURE 32
Young foliage and male flowers (above), female flowers (below), of European larch, with a straight-scaled cone, spring ($\times\frac{1}{4}$).

31

Larix kaempferi and Larix × eurolepis

This larch grows wild on the mountains of Japan. It was introduced to Britain in 1861, and began to attract attention as a plantation tree about 1910. Nowadays it is more widely planted than the European kind because it grows faster and seems better adapted to our variable climate. It is easily known by its dark orange, purple, or rust-red twigs, which look very striking during the winter months. Its needles are bluish green in summer, fading to orange in autumn. The cone scales are bent back or reflexed at the tip, so that each cone looks like a little rosette (Figure 35). The timber of Japanese larch is similar to that of the European kind, and has comparable strength properties. This tree is often planted on old woodlands, particularly cleared coppices, where it is required to get a timber crop established quickly, ahead of the regrowth from the stumps of felled trees or cleared bushes. The transplant illustrated in Figure 34 is aged 2 years, or '1 + 1'.

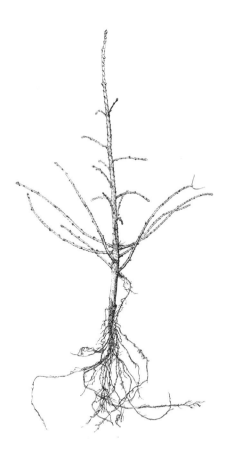

FIGURE 33
One-year-old Japanese larch *Larix kaempferi* seedling, winter. The early needles are evergreen (×⅓).

FIGURE 34
A sturdy 2-year-old (1+1) Japanese larch transplant, winter (×⅓).

Hybrid larch, *Larix × eurolepis* Henry, first arose through the chance cross-pollination of female flowers of Japanese larch by male flowers of the European kind. This happened on the estate of the Duke of Atholl, at Dunkeld in Tayside, about 1904. Nowadays most of the seed for raising it comes from seed orchards set up by the Forestry Commission, in which selected trees of each kind are grown in alternate rows, to increase the probability of cross-fertilisation.

This 'first-cross' shows to a remarkable degree the property called *hybrid vigour*. It grows faster than either parent, and will do reasonably well under poorer conditions of infertile soil or greater exposure than its parents can stand. It is not illustrated here because its characters are variable, but intermediate between those of the Japanese and the European kinds. A whole plantation can often be picked out from this circumstance, but it is less easy to be sure of any one individual tree.

FIGURE 35
Foliage and cones of Japanese larch. Note reflexed cone scales, and solitary needles at lower twig tip, summer ($\times\frac{1}{4}$).

Metasequoia glyptostroboides

There was a sensation when it became known in 1945 that this tree had been discovered in 1941 growing in central China. It had long been familiar as a fossil widely spaced over the world in rocks 100 million years old and there was no indication that it might have survived anywhere. Seeds were sent around the world in January 1948 and the biggest trees in most of the major gardens date from 1949 plantings from this seed. In Britain these are now (1983) 20–25m tall and 50–60cm in diameter of bole and now growing in diameter even faster, but height growth has slowed from the earlier 1–1.3m a year as they have grown out of the damp, sheltering woodland surround that they need for best growth. In warmer, damper parts of the USA several are (1981) 30m tall and one is 32m while another had a bole 1.25m through.

There are Dawn redwoods in most of the large and in many small gardens in England, but fewer in the north and in Wales, and it is scare in Scotland. Usually it is a shapely tree, slender conic with numerous light branches but some are broad at the base. The foliage is deciduous, like that of the Swamp cypress (see page 57), another redwood; but unlike that, it is of broad rectangular leaves set in opposite pairs on shoots which also arise in opposite pairs, yet like the Swamp cypress, however, in autumn both the leaves and the minor shoots bearing them are shed. The leaves emerge a month before those of the Swamp cypress, in late March and shoot growth begins in the last week of April. The leaves are on greyish pink shoots when growth is strong and are light green, paler beneath, until late autumn when they turn yellow, pink orange and then deep red. The sexes are on the same tree but the males require hotter summers than we have and have not been seen here, but even young trees yielded numerous cones in the hot summer of 1959, when they were 10 years old, and many

FIGURE 36

Dawn redwood *Metasequoia glyptostroboides* foliage (×½). Leaves and shoots in opposite pairs are both shed in the autumn.

more in 1976. The cones are green, somewhat egg-shaped 3–4cm long on 5cm stalks.

In 1979 a second import of seed was brought from China, but until then all new planting had been of cuttings raised from the 1948 trees. Cuttings can be hardwood, taken in January and February or softwood taken in June or July and inserted, after a dusting with rooting hormone powder, in an open sandy soil. The softwood cuttings have a polythene bag tied over the pot to prevent the soft foliage from drying out.

As well as having a remarkable history, the Dawn redwood is a botanical oddity in the way it bears its lateral buds. Throughout the plant kingdom lateral buds are axillary – that is they lie in the angle between the main stem and a side-shoot or leaf. In this tree (and occasionally in the Coast redwood) most of the buds are below or behind the side-shoot not in the angle above it.

Dawn redwoods thrive in warm, sheltered, damp sites and dislike exposure and dry soils. The first leaves out are often scorched by late frosts but this has no lasting effect and the shoots scarcely emerging until May are rarely affected. As with the Ginkgo, there are no pests here which have ever lived on Dawn redwood and it remains healthy in foliage but can be killed by Honey fungus.

Picea abies

The Norway spruce is the usual Christmas tree, but it is also one of the world's leading timber producers. It grows wild over most of northern and central Europe, and on mountain ranges further south, but it is not native to Britain. It was introduced at some unknown date, certainly by the mid-16th century, and has been planted on a growing scale ever since. Though self-sown seedlings are sometimes found, nearly all our spruces are raised artificially from seed in nursery beds.

All the spruces are easily known because their needles stand on tiny pegs (see page 8). The Norway spruce is readily told from the Sitka spruce by its mid-green needles, which are pointed but less sharply so. Spruce trees have a thin bark which appears smooth in general outline, scaly but not fibrous or furrowed, and has a roughish surface due to small irregularities. In the Norway spruce this bark, though greyish-brown in general colour, always has a reddish or rusty tint that aids identification; in fact the Germans call it the 'red-spruce'. The base of the trunk often spreads out in ridges or buttresses. The male flowers are clusters of yellow anthers, borne in May, which soon fall. The female flowers are greenish, oval structures that ripen rapidly, between spring and autumn, into very distinctive long, cylindrical brown cones, which have straight scales and always hang downwards when ripe.

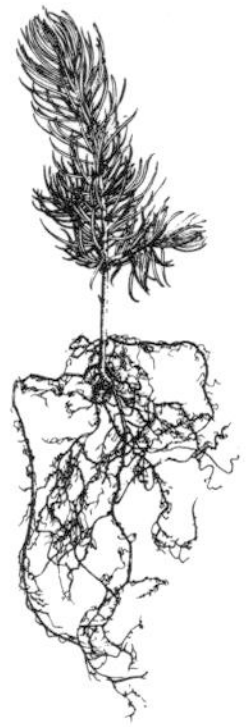

FIGURE 37
One-year-old Norway spruce *Picea abies* seedling, winter (×¼).

FIGURE 38
Norway spruce transplant aged 3 years (2+1), winter (×¼).

FIGURE 39
Male flowers and foliage of Norway spruce, spring ($\times\frac{1}{4}$).

FIGURE 40
Female flowers amid foliage of Norway spruce, spring ($\times\frac{1}{4}$).

The seeds that fall from these cones in spring are very small; each seed sits in a little cup at the base of its wing, to which it is only lightly attached. The resulting seedling is quite tiny also, rarely growing over 8cm in its first year; so the forester leaves it for 2 years in the seedbed. It then spends 1-2 years more in a transplant bed before going to the forest. A good root system is needed because spruces are planted with their roots spread out in shallow fashion, just below the ground surface, beneath an over-turned turf, or beneath the slice of turf turned over by a plough. Roots set more deeply would make no progress. Early growth is slow, but eventually the trees grow taller rapidly, and their stems bulk out fast, so that the total yield of timber is high.

The timbers of all the spruces are much alike and their proper-ties are further described under 'Sitka spruce', on page 41. Much Norway spruce timber is imported from Scandinavia and Russia under the trade name of 'whitewood' or 'white deal', and it is widely used in the building, box making and joinery industries.

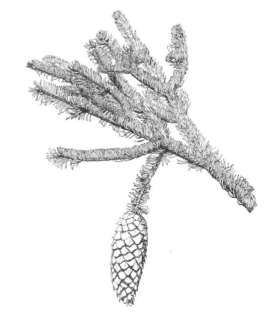

FIGURE 41
Norway spruce cone and foliage, autumn ($\times\frac{1}{10}$).

SERBIAN SPRUCE

Picea omorika

This botanical anomaly has been found to be unusually useful as a tree in small gardens and parks, even in towns. It was discovered high in the Drina Valley in Yugoslavia in 1875 and is a flat-needled spruce, thousands of miles from all the others, which grow round the Pacific shores and through China to the Himalayas. All the European and eastern American spruces have needles nearly square in cross-section. It is an adaptable tree, growing on any soil from limestones to acid peats and it comes into leaf too late to be damaged by frosts. It withstands polluted air to a greater degree than other spruces, and it remains so slender in the crown that a specimen 20m tall can be acceptable in a very small garden.

The shoots are thinly covered in pale long hairs and bear leaves rich green above with two blue-white broad bands beneath. Some trees are slender-conic with gracefully downswept short branches and some are narrow columns with short, more level branching and upturned terminal shoots. Female flowers are borne around the top of the crown from an early age, bright red, ripening to small spindle-shaped cones. Male flowers, large for a spruce are borne on hanging shoots in the lower crown and are globules 8mm across, bright red until about to shed pollen.

There are a few forest stands on a variety of soils in a number of forests and they yield a remarkably high volume of timber, partly because the narrow crowns allow a higher density of stems than other trees can tolerate and thus they flourish. The only disadvantage the tree has is a tendency to a short life. Many trees succumb to Honey fungus while quite young and old trees have a marked tendency to become thin in foliage, make very little growth for some years and then to die. As a possibly short-term tree for a confined space it is among the best of all conifers.

FIGURE 42
Serbian spruce *Picea omorika* foliage ($\times\frac{1}{2}$). Trees with the narrowest crowns have the densest foliage, with many leaves upcurved.

Picea pungens

This tree ranges over the eastern crests of the Rocky Mountain system from Wyoming to Colorado and is variable in colour. Many trees have deep blue-green foliage while others are pale, nearer blue-grey. A very blue form was selected in 1877 and grown in a Surrey nursery from which grafts were sent out. These are var. *glauca* and can be raised from seed. In Holland 10 very blue trees were selected and some of them grafted in large numbers. These have brighter, more white foliage than var. *glauca*, usually deep orange or purple shoots and grow a little more slowly. They are the cultivar 'Koster' and need to be grafted to keep true to name. Together these Blue Colorado spruces are among the commonest decorative conifers planted in the smaller gardens and parks. They prefer the damper west of Britain to the east, where they grow rather slowly and suffer from Green spruce aphid *Elatobium* and red spider mite.

Cones are borne crowded around the tops of the older trees and they are very like those of Sitka spruce, short-cylindric, parchment-like crinkled scales, cream or pale brown. The needles on new growth radiate all round the shoot or, in 'Koster' tend to stand above it and are stiff and sharply pointed. The bark is purplish grey-black, sometimes dark brown, and always very scaly.

FIGURE 43
Foliage of Blue Colorado spruce *Picea pungens* var. *glauca* (×½).
The leaves radiate from the shoot and are stiff and spined.

Picea sitchensis

Many spruces from Asia and America have been grown experimentally in Britain, as possible timber trees, but only one has proved a marked success. This is the Sitka spruce, named after the small seaport Sitka in southern Alaska. Its natural range extends down the western seaboard of North America, from Kodiak Island to California. The seed needed for raising trees in the British Isles is often imported from British Columbia, Washington and Oregon as those strains grow vigorously in our climate. Sitka spruce is fairly easily known because all its needles have a bluish or slaty-grey tint. They end in a really sharp point, which makes the foliage rough to touch, and rules it out for use as a Christmas tree. The cones are very distinctive, being quite short and cream or pale brown in colour; each of the thin scales has a crinkly edge, unlike that on other common conifers. The winged seeds are remarkably small, and the resulting seedlings are usually kept for 2 years in the seedbeds. The transplant illustrated is 4 years old, and has the good root system needed for shallow planting. Sitka spruce bark is thin and appears smooth to the eye, but is rough to the touch. It is greyish-brown in colour, and often breaks away in shallow plates. The base of the trunk is often buttressed.

FIGURE 44
One-year-old Sitka spruce *Picea sitchensis* seedling ($\times\frac{1}{2}$).

FIGURE 45
Four-year-old (2+2) Sitka spruce transplant ($\times\frac{1}{4}$).

FIGURE 46
Spray of Sitka spruce foliage, with drooping crinkly-scaled cones ($\times\frac{1}{6}$).

slight one between the paler springwood and darker summerwood of each annual ring. It is even in texture, easily worked and holds nails well, and it is strong in relation to its size and weight. It has no natural durability out-of-doors, but the sapwood takes preservative and so logs can be used for fencing or telegraph poles. A good deal goes to the mines as pit props. Much is used for making boxes and packing cases, while there is an even greater demand in house-building, as joists, rafters and flooring. Selected material is used for joinery and ladder-making.

Spruce timber has proved very suitable for making various kinds of manufactured board, such as wood chipboard, insulation board, and hardboard, and much home-grown wood goes to the board factories. The greatest world demand, however, now comes from the paper makers, who prefer spruce to all other timbers, no matter what process they use for making their paper pulp. It is also preferred by the makers of cellulose, cellophane and rayon fabrics. Much home-grown spruce wood now goes to newsprint mills.

For many years the Forestry Commission has planted more Sitka spruce than any other individual kind of tree. This is because it is well suited to the peaty hills and moors in Scotland, Wales and the north and the west of England where much poor grazing land has become available for afforestation. It enjoys a high rainfall, but in the south and east of Britain, where rainfall drops below 1000mm a year, it is not really at home, so there it is seldom planted. On good ground in the west it starts growth slowly, but soon increases in height by as much as 1–1.3m a year. At the same time its girth grows rapidly, and as a rule it yields a greater volume of timber, in a given time, than any other tree. Further, it grows upright despite severe exposure, even to salt-laden winds blowing straight in from the sea. In central and northern Scotland there are many trees, dating usually from 1850–1860 which are now among the biggest trees in Britain, 50–55m tall and 2m or more in diameter.

The timber yielded so readily by Sitka spruce is very like that of the Norway spruce or 'whitewood'. As the name suggests, it is pale creamy brown, or almost white in colour. No colour difference can be seen between sapwood and heartwood, and only a

LODGEPOLE PINE

Pinus contorta

Many kinds of introduced pines have been grown on an experimental scale to see if they would thrive on poor soil in the west of Britain, where both the native Scots pine and the Corsican pine are unsatisfactory as timber crops. The one that has proved most useful, in Wales, northern Scotland, north-west England, and also throughout Ireland, is the Lodgepole pine. As a wild tree this grows in western North America, from Alaska down to California, both along the coast and on the inland mountain ranges; it is important in practice to choose a provenance or local strain well suited to the climate where the plantations will be established. It is called Lodgepole pine because the Indians chose its straight stems to support their lodges or wigwams.

FIGURE 47
One-year-old seedling of Lodgepole pine *Pinus contorta*, winter (×$\frac{1}{2}$).

FIGURE 48
Lodgepole pine transplant aged 3 years (1+2), winter (×$\frac{1}{3}$).

In appearance the foliage of Lodgepole pine is rather like that of Scots pine, but its needles have a mid-green tint, not a blue-green one. The bark is quite different from that of Scots pine and differs between those from the coastal areas, in which it becomes rich brown small square plates divided by fissures, and the inland forms in which it is brown and scaly. The cone, as our pictures show, is somewhat egg-shaped, and each scale carries a small, sharp, prickle.

The foliage tends to be dense, with much overlapping of needles. The timber resembles that of Scots pine and has similar uses. Because of its remarkable tolerance of poor soils, including peaty moorlands, in our wetter and cloudier western districts, Lodgepole pine is now very widely planted there. Under comparable conditions it grows somewhat faster than does Scots pine.

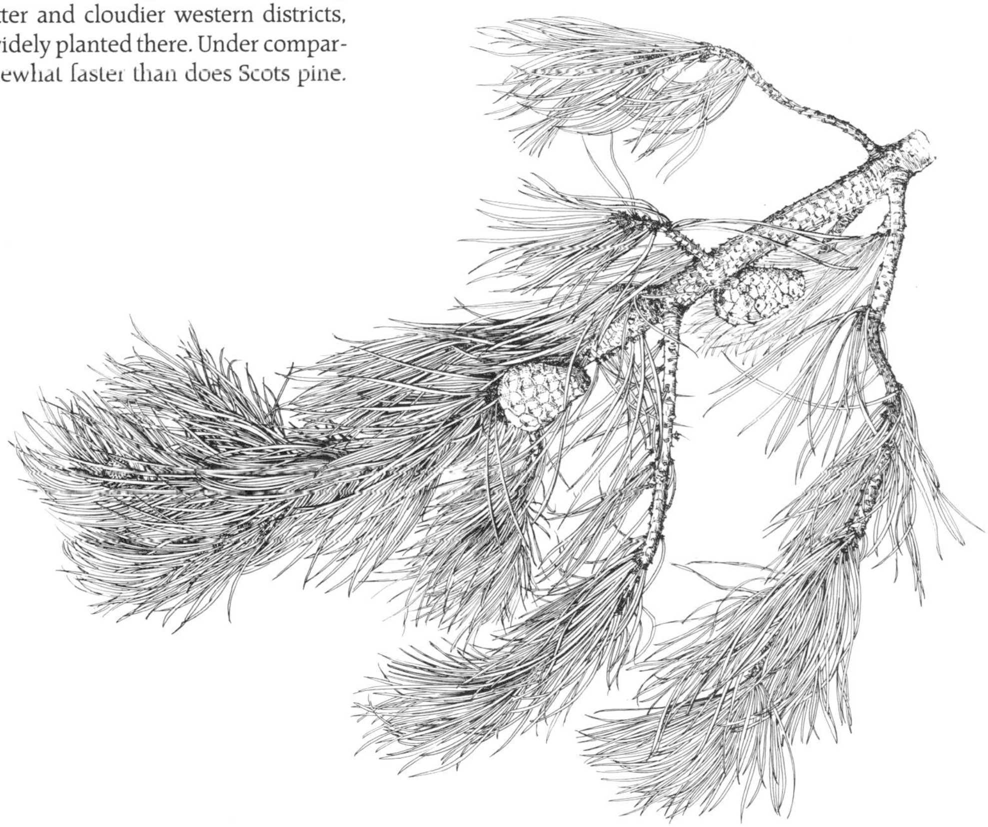

FIGURE 49
Cone and foliage of Lodgepole pine, winter ($\times\frac{1}{4}$).

CORSICAN PINE

Pinus nigra var. maritima

The Corsican pine is one of a number of local races of the Black pine, *Pinus nigra*, a tree with a wide distribution over the south and east of Europe. It has been selected for timber production in Britain because it grows fast and has a remarkably straight trunk, with light branches. Another local race, the Austrian pine, variety *nigra* (Am.), which has *straight* needles, is mentioned next.

The true Corsican pine is native only to the Mediterranean island of Corsica, where it reaches great size and age. It is only satisfactory as a timber crop in the south and the Midlands of England, the coastal fringe of south Wales, and along the east coast up to the north of Scotland. These are all districts of low summer rainfall, with correspondingly high summer temperatures and duration of sunshine; in the wetter, cloudier districts of the north and west this Mediterranean tree does not really thrive. Our most extensive plantations are in East Anglia, especially at Thetford Chase and at Aldewood near Ipswich, but Corsican pine also grows well at Culbin near Nairn on the Moray Firth.

FIGURE 50
One-year-old seedling of Corsican pine *Pinus nigra* var. *maritima*, winter (×1).

FIGURE 51
Corsican pine transplant aged 3 years (2+1), winter (×$\frac{1}{4}$).

Corsican pine is easily known by the length of its needles, commonly 8cm long, by their distinctive *twist* which is well shown in our foliage sketch, and by their colour, which is a greyish-green or sage-green. Another key point is the shape of the terminal bud, which is broad at the base but narrows suddenly to a sharp point (Scots and Lodgepole pines bear long, blunt buds). The cones are larger than those of other common pines, shining mid-brown when ripe, and always one-sided or oblique in shape. The seeds are about twice as big as those of Scots pine. The bark is grey or greyish-black to greyish-pink, but never red, and this explains the name of 'black' pine; it is thick and fibrous, and is broken up by deep furrows on old trees.

The pictures of a 1-year-old seedling and a 3-year-old (2+1) transplant show a feature that causes much concern to the forester. Corsican pine roots are remarkably long and slender, and hence they cannot readily take up enough moisture when the young trees are transplanted. For this reason foresters prefer to move young Corsican pine trees during the winter months, such as February, when the ground is moist and water loss from transpiration is low, or in midsummer when the top growth has ceased but the roots are growing fast. Once established, Corsican pine can withstand severe drought, as is shown by its success on dry sandy soils in regions of low rainfall.

The timber resembles that of Scots pine, but where the two are grown under similar conditions the Corsican pine grows faster and forms wider annual rings; while in logs of comparable sizes the Corsican pine shows less heartwood. It is used for the same purposes as Scots pine.

FIGURE 52
Foliage and opening 2-year-old cones of Corsican pine ($\times\frac{1}{6}$).

Pinus nigra var. nigra

Although the Austrian pine is the form found in the eastern Alps and south to Yugoslavia and is botanically the basic form of Black pine, it was the last to be introduced to Britain in 1838. It is very commonly planted where its rugged health in polluted air, on the poorest soils, at high exposure, and on chalklands, is exploited. It is most common in the screen-belts around old gardens now engulfed in towns, on railway embankments and by the east coasts.

It is distinguishable from the Corsican pine by its shorter, straight or incurved needles markedly in whorls with bare shoot between, where male flowers were borne. The foliage is also much blacker and more dense, and the bark is nearly black and even more flaky on coarse ridges. Another difference is the crown form but this is highly variable. Some trees are obviously Austrian with strong rising branches or many boles, but a few do grow single, straight boles. They are distinguished from Corsican by longer branches rather drooping with short, dense, black foliage.

Establishment is rapid for some 10 years after which growth in height becomes slow. The timber is coarse-grained and knotty and has no value.

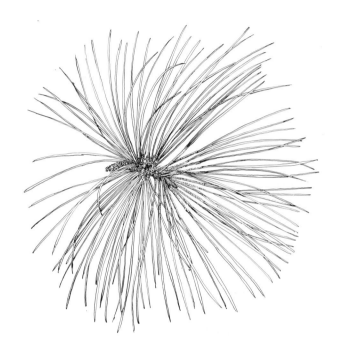

FIGURE 53
Austrian pine *Pinus nigra* var. *nigra* foliage ($\times\frac{1}{4}$). The paired needles have a conspicuous basal sheath. The foliage is set in dense branches separated by short bare lengths of shoot.

MONTEREY PINE

Pinus radiata

This remarkable tree grows wild only in two very small areas by the coast of California, where it never makes a big tree. In southern and western England it may reach 30m in 40 years and the numerous trees planted 1850–1880 are now immense. It is the common shelter-tree of Cornwall and much of the south-west and is frequent inland, making a very big rough tree particularly in mid-Kent, but there are few in Scotland.

The needles are in threes, slender and bright grassy green although big trees look black from a distance. The slender cylindric buds begin to lengthen in February in the south-west and many trees carry quantities of male flowers, bright yellow when shedding pollen in March or April. The cones are held strongly on the tree for 50 years or more but are frequently found beneath big trees on branches which have been broken off, clustered in threes. They are heavily woody and have an oblique base, the scales on the outer side being expanded into projections. A spell in a hot oven is needed to extract the seeds. The bark is at first smooth and grey, then is rapidly divided by long, deep, pale brown fissures and on old trees it is slightly purplish black with ridges standing 15cm cut from the deep, wide fissures, and scaling coarsely.

The Monterey pine occasionally seeds itself but is established with difficulty unless small, 2-year-old plants are used and planting is done in early autumn or in midsummer. It grows well on almost any soil including poor sands but on thin soils over chalk, after a rapid start, it becomes unhealthy and yellow before it is 40-years-old. The extremely rapid growth shows some promise for plantation use in southern England, and trials are being grown using improved strains from New Zealand.

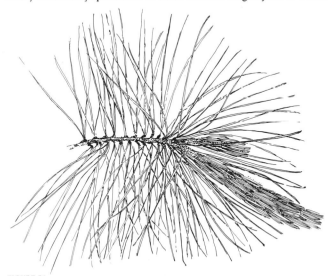

FIGURE 54
Monterey pine *Pinus radiata* foliage ($\times\frac{1}{2}$). New shoots start to expand in January in mild western areas and in March in the east and inland.

FIGURE 55
Monterey pine cone ($\times\frac{1}{4}$). Firmly fixed on the tree, the cones remain on old branches when these are blown off, and in the natural stands, await a fire while on the tree.

Pinus sylvestris

The Scots pine, our only native timber-producing conifer, is now found in its wild state only in Scotland and – very locally – northern England. But it has been planted everywhere and it grows readily from self-sown seed on heaths in many southern counties. It can at once be recognised as a pine because, except on the youngest seedlings, all its needles are set in pairs (see sketch, page 7). You can tell it apart from our other common pines by the colour and length of these needles; they are blue-green and relatively short – about 4cm long. Another key feature is the bark; Scots pine is the only common tree to develop a distinctively orange-red coloration. As each portion of the trunk or branches reaches an age of about 10 years, the grey outer bark falls away and this striking red shade is exposed. On old trunks the bark, now pinkish grey, is often divided up by irregular cracks into broad flat plates.

Male flowers, illustrated on page 49, consist of clusters of golden anthers, set some way back from the tips of the twigs; they shed clouds of pollen in May, and then wither. The female flowers appear at the same time, at the very tip of a newly expanded shoot; they are tiny, crimson tinted globes. After fertilisation, they grow slowly during the next year into brown structures no larger

FIGURE 58
Scots pine transplant aged 3 years (1+2) suitable for forest planting, winter ($\times\frac{1}{4}$).

FIGURE 56
First season seedling of Scots pine *Pinus sylvestris* ($\times\frac{2}{3}$). Whorl of several seed-leaves followed by solitary juvenile needles.

FIGURE 57
One-year-old seedling of Scots pine, winter ($\times\frac{1}{4}$).

48

Specimen
in colour

D1135686

1

2

Plate 1:
Silver fir *(Abies alba).*

Plate 2:
Grand fir *(Abies grandis).*

Plate 3:
Noble fir cone *(Abies procera).*

Plate 4:
Noble fir *(Abies procera).*

3

4

M. Nimmo

Plate 5:
Caucasian fir
(*Abies nordmanniana*).

Plate 6:
Chile pine or
Monkey puzzle
(*Araucaria araucana*).

Plate 7 (inset):
Monkey puzzle cone
and foliage (*Araucaria araucana*).

5

8

9

26748

21799

10

11

12

Plate 8:
Incense cedar
(Calocedrus decurrens).

Plate 9:
Atlas cedar
(Cedrus atlantica).

Plate 10:
Deodar
(Cedrus deodara).

Plate 11:
Blue Atlas cedar
(Cedrus atlantica
var. *glauca)*.

Plate 12:
Cedar of Lebanon
(Cedrus libani).

13

14

15

12298

16

15585

17

Plate 13:
Lawson cypress varieties
(*Chamaecyparis
lawsoniana*).

Plate 14:
Lawson cypress
(*Chamaecyparis
lawsoniana*), foliage
and flowers.

Plate 15:
Leyland cypress
(× *Cupressocyparis
leylandii*).

Plate 16:
Monterey cypress
(*Cupressus
macrocarpa*).

Plate 17:
Smooth Arizona
cypress (*Cupressus
glabra*).

26696

18

30171

19

Plate 18:
Maidenhair tree
(Ginkgo biloba).

Plate 19:
Golden Chinese
juniper *(Juniperus
chinensis* 'Aurea').

Plate 20:
Common juniper
(*Juniperus communis*).
A young tree on the
chalk downs.

Plate 21 (inset):
Common juniper
(*Juniperus communis*),
foliage and berries

20733

12830

Plate 22:
Japanese larch *(Larix kaempferi)*, in winter

Plate 23:
Hybrid larch cone
(Larix × eurolepis).

Plate 24:
European larch
(Larix decidua).

Plate 25:
Dawn redwood
(Metasequoia glyptostroboides), with
Giant sequoia
(Sequoiadendron giganteum).

22

24

25

6108

13319

26

27

Plate 26:
Norway spruce
(Picea abies).

Plate 27:
Serbian spruce
(Picea omorika).

28

29

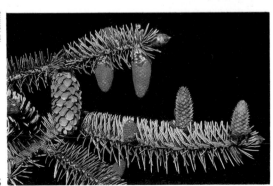

30

Plate 28:
Blue Colorado spruce
(*Picea pungens*
var. *glauca*).

Plate 29:
Sitka spruce
plantation (*Picea
sitchensis*).

Plate 30:
Sitka spruce (*Picea
sitchensis*), foliage,
flowers and cone.

Plate 31:
Corsican pine *(Pinus nigra* var. *maritima),* plantation.

Plate 32:
Lodgepole pine *(Pinus contorta).*

Plate 33:
Austrian pine *(Pinus nigra* var. *nigra).*

32

33

M. Nimmo

M. Nimmo

Plate 34:
Monterey pine
(Pinus radiata).

Plate 35 (inset):
Monterey pine *(Pinus radiata).*
Two-year-old cones.

Plate 36:
Scots pine *(Pinus sylvestris).*

Plate 37:
Bhutan pine
(Pinus wallichiana).

34

36

37

15383

Plate 38:
Douglas fir
(*Pseudotsuga
menziesii*).

Plate 39 (inset):
Douglas fir
(*Pseudotsuga
menziesii*), flowers.

Plate 40:
Coast redwood
(*Sequoia
sempervirens*).

38

17917

21893

M. Nimmo

Plate 41:
Swamp cypress
(Taxodium distichum).

Plate 42:
Yew *(Taxus baccata)*
(with Whitebeam),
on the chalk downs.

Plate 43:
Yew *(Taxus baccata)*,
foliage and berries.

41

42

43

Plate 44:
Irish yew
(Taxus baccata
'Fastigiata'*).*

44

45

46

Plate 45:
Western red cedar
(Thuja plicata).

Plate 46:
Western hemlock
(Tsuga heterophylla).

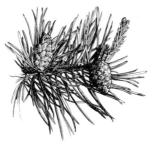

FIGURE 59
Male flowers (clusters of anthers, left) and female flowers (small spheres at right branch tip), on a Scots pine branch that is just expanding new needles in May. The cone below is 2 years old (×⅛).

than a pea (Figure 60, right tip); they need 2 years for full ripening. Mature cones which ripen one or two whorls, or annual growth stages, back from the tip of the shoot, owing to its continued growth, are at first green with tightly-shut scales. When seed is needed, they are gathered in this state during the winter. Their symmetrical, 'pointed-cone' shape helps the tree's identification; each scale bears a knob but no points. In spring they turn brown and the scales open to release the winged seeds, shown on page 65. As in all pines, the seed is lightly held in a curved 'claw' at the base of the wing.

When the seed sprouts, the seed case is raised above ground on a long stalk; it soon falls off and exposes a whorl of about eight seed-leaves, which are visible at the base of the foliage in the seedling sketches. As the shoot develops, solitary needles are borne, during the first season only; Figure 56, and Figure 57. The transplant picture shows a tree 3 years old; it is a '1+2' transplant that has spent one year in a seedbed and 2 years in a transplant bed after 'lining out'. All its early solitary needles have fallen, and only paired needles remain. This example shows a sturdy stem and a good 'balance' between shoot growth and bushy fibrous roots.

Though the Scots pine can be grown nearly anywhere in the British Isles, it is most successful as a timber tree in the warmer and drier districts towards the south and east. Its timber has a distinct reddish heartwood surrounded by pale-brown sapwood; it is resinous, but not naturally durable. In addition to the home-grown supply, very large quantities are imported from northern Europe, and this material is known in the timber trade as 'red-wood' or 'red deal'. Scots pine timber can be readily treated with creosote or similar preservatives, and is then well suited to use out of doors as telegraph poles, railway sleepers, and fencing. Under the cover of a roof, it serves as a leading building timber, being used for joists, rafters, and flooring; other uses include sheds, pit props, box making, wood wool, wall board, and paper pulp.

The timber of pines can usually be told apart from that of other conifers by the *absence* of small knots between the main knot groups; this is because pines bear all their branches in simple whorls, usually one whorl a year, without small intermediate shoots.

Old Scots pine trees, but not young ones, can usually be picked out by their rugged, irregular upper branches, resembling in outline a broadleaved tree.

The natural range of the Scots pine includes all northern Europe, northern Asia, Spain and Asia Minor. Seed of native Scottish strains, from either the west or the east of Scotland according to local climate, is preferred for present-day planting in Britain. The Forestry Commission has within its care some remarkably fine expanses of the old native Caledonian pine forest, notably at Glen Affric and the Glen More Forest Park in the Highland Region of Scotland, and at Rannoch Forest in Tayside. Younger plantations of impressive extent will be found at Thetford Chase in East Anglia, in the New Forest, and at Cannock Chase in Staffordshire.

FIGURE 60
Scots pine foliage with a 1-year-old unripe cone at the branch tip, and a 2-year-old ripe cone one whorl further down, March (×⅒).

BHUTAN PINE

Pinus wallichiana

For no obvious reason, this is the only 5-needle pine seen frequently in parks and outer suburban gardens. It is shapely and very vigorous as a young tree but with age it grows a broad crown, bears a heavy load of cones and soon deteriorates. The bark is deep brown scaly ridges divided by orange fissures. The shoot, unlike the slender, slightly hairy one of the Weymouth pine, *Pinus strobus* for which it is often mistaken, is stout, smooth and bloomed blue-grey. The needles are 15cm long and hang gracefully, showing blue-white inner surfaces and deep green outer sides. Young trees growing 1m a year may start to bear flowers, the females pale pink-purple globes on 2cm stalks, at the tip of the

year's growth, the males small and egg-shaped strung along side shoots rather sparsely below the sector bearing needles. The females mature in their first year, to bright green, resin-encrusted banana-shaped cones which turn dark brown as they become woody and the scales open. They are in twos and threes and are usually numerous. The Bhutan or Himalayan blue pine grows in the western Himalayas and was first sent here in 1823. Many were planted in around 1860 and these are the big trees, around 30m × 1m diameter which are seen in many big gardens and estates dying back at the top and shedding branches.

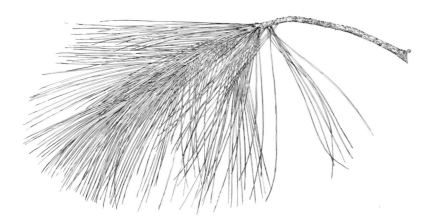

FIGURE 61
Bhutan pine *Pinus wallichiana* foliage. The stout smooth shoot, dark green bloomed violet, distinguishes this from other five-needle pines with long needles ($\times\frac{1}{3}$).

FIGURE 62
Bhutan pine cone. Bright blue-green in early summer, it becomes woody and brown in the autumn ($\times\frac{1}{3}$).

DOUGLAS FIR

Pseudotsuga menziesii

This beautiful conifer is named after David Douglas, the Scottish botanist who, in 1827, sent the first seed home to Britain. Its scientific name commemorates another Scottish botanist, Archibald Menzies, who discovered the tree in 1791. Its homeland extends down the western side of North America, from British Columbia to California; most of the seed we sow in Britain comes from the neighbourhood of Vancouver Island in British Columbia. There it forms magnificent forests, outgrowing other conifers and often reaching 75m in height. Here in Britain it has become one of our tallest trees with one specimen at Inver, Perth, 60m tall in 1982 and many small stands in N. Scotland with trees over 55m even when only 100 years old. In Somerset, the New Forest, north Wales and Argyll there are stands with dominant trees 46–52m tall.

A few simple features identify the foliage of Douglas fir. The solitary needles do not stand on pegs, and if they are pulled away they leave a smooth round scar on the twig's surface. The buds are brown, scaly, and taper to a point; they resemble the buds of a beech tree, but are not so thin; these buds mark the Douglas fir out from the Silver firs, described on pages 10 to 14. The cone is very distinctive; it is egg shaped and hangs downwards, and outside every scale there is a straight three-pointed bract found on no

FIGURE 63
One-year-old seedling of Douglas fir *Pseudotsuga menziesii*, winter (×⅓).

FIGURE 64
Douglas fir transplant aged 3 years (2+1). Note the slender pointed buds, winter (×⅓).

other tree. The bark is at first greyish-black and smooth and bears resin blisters; later it becomes very thick and deeply fissured, and shows orange-brown tints in the cracks.

The male flowers of Douglas fir are clusters of yellow stamens which open in May and soon wither thereafter. The female flowers, borne near the branch tips, are short cylindric, varying from bright red and pink to pale green; they ripen rapidly to brown cones, which start to drop their winged seeds during the following autumn. Seedlings grow rapidly and are occasionally transplanted when 1-year-old. The picture shows a 3-year-old (2+1) transplant. Douglas fir is widely planted, but usually on the better ground, not in extreme exposure or on very poor soil. It is often used in the replanting of felled woodland; it stands light shade in youth so is sometimes given the protection of a light cover of birch trees. On good ground it grows fast, right from the start, and produces timber at a rate which rivals the spruces.

The timber of Douglas fir is marketed under that name in Canada and America, but when it is imported into Britain it is sold under the trade names of 'Oregon pine' and 'Columbian pine', probably because it bears a strong resemblance to true ·pine timbers. It has a well-marked reddish-brown heartwood that contrasts strongly with its pale creamy-brown sapwood. The annual rings are always clearly visible, for broad zones of dark brown summerwood alternate with the paler springwood. The timber works well and has good strength properties. It is used in building and general construction work, just as pine would be, and also in engineering as imported material is available in large sizes. Strong plywood is obtained from the big logs available in North America. Our home-grown trees are used for fencing, pit props, telegraph poles, sawmill timber, and paper pulp.

FIGURE 65
Foliage spray of Douglas fir with female flower near the tip, May (×¼).

FIGURE 66
Douglas fir cones ripening amid the foliage in autumn. Note three-pointed bracts and the position of the cones, one whorl back from the branch tips (×⅓).

Sequoia sempervirens

This is the only tree in the world to make groves of trees over 100m tall. Many such groves are preserved in the 800km belt of native Coast redwood in the narrow strip behind the coast and among low hills from a few kilometres into Oregon southwards in California to beyond Monterey. One such grove contains 'Tallest Tree', the tallest in the world at 112m but it is dying back at the top and better groves further south have many green topped trees 110m tall and still growing.

This tree was first sent in 1843 but large imports of seed came in 1850 and after, and trees of this age are frequent in old gardens everywhere. They have not thrived in eastern or nothern England but there are many huge specimens in western England, in Wales and central and northern Scotland. Two of these are now 45m tall and many have boles 1.8– 2.0m in diameter. Growth in height can be remarkably rapid in damp sheltered woods for many years – some in the New Forest were 29m in 27 years – but when shelter is outgrown, growth in height almost ceases.

The hard, evergreen leaves, banded white beneath, lie each

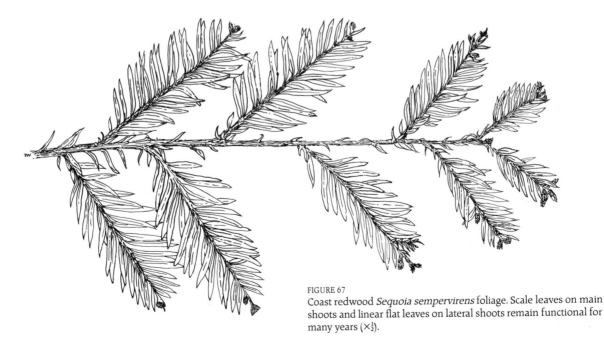

FIGURE 67
Coast redwood *Sequoia sempervirens* foliage. Scale leaves on main shoots and linear flat leaves on lateral shoots remain functional for many years ($\times\frac{1}{2}$).

side of the green-scaled shoot and often scorch brown in dry freezing winds but the tree is little affected. Male flowers grow in the autumn at the tips of small shoots. They are 5mm droplet-shaped and whitish yellow, shedding pollen in February. Female flowers are tiny green rosettes ripening to 8mm globular, spined cones, borne profusely but not often carrying fertile seed since February is not usually dry enough for the pollen to be shed and more frequently a frost kills the flowers just before they shed. Seed imported from America gives a good quantity of strong seedlings usually including a number with markedly superior vigour. After one or two years in the seedbed, depending on the density of plants, for crowding must be avoided, these are trans-planted and the best are ready for planting out by the end of the year. Cuttings root readily, if slowly, but those from side-shoots take many years to grow into sturdy plants and strong vertical shoots are quicker. These may often be obtained from the sprouts around the base of a big tree. It is unusual among conifers in this sprouting at the base and it is shown best when a tree is felled and a circle of sprouts, using the big root-system of the old tree, grows very rapidly to make a ring of trees. Such 'family circles' are left in the cut-over native stands, to be harvested as second growth, but

FIGURE 68
Coast redwood cone after shedding seed (×1).

in a garden it is far better to single out the best placed or strongest and remove the others so that a single new tree grows to replace the old. In this form of sprout on an old root-system, Coast redwood will grow in denser shade than any other tree, and seedling trees grow in quite heavy shade too, but will need more light as they grow, to maintain their vigour.

GIANT SEQUOIA

Sequoiadendron giganteum

The world's greatest trees with regard to volume of timber were found in 1852 by a hunter employed to feed labourers during the Californian goldrush which began in 1849. The first seeds and foliage were brought to Britain in late 1853 and the tree was then named after the Duke who had died 2 years before, 'Wellingtonia'. To the rest of the world it is the Giant sequoia, Big Tree or Sierra redwood. It grows only in 70 small and two large groves scattered along the foothills on the western flanks of the Sierra Nevada, all now protected. There were thousands of trees raised from the first seeds between 1854 and 1862 and these tower out of gardens and parks, in avenues, clumps and rows in all parts of Britain. It lives for over 3000 years in California and although it is unlikely to last so long with us, it is healthy and never known to blow down, nor is the timber wanted, so the original trees are mostly still growing. A few have died with Honey fungus and a few have been torn apart by lightning but those in England are mostly struck

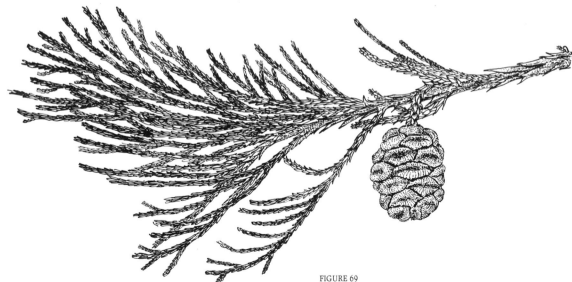

FIGURE 69
Giant sequoia *Sequoiadendron giganteum.* The hard foliage, harsh to the touch, varies on different trees from dark shiny green to dull blue-grey ($\times\frac{2}{3}$).

from time to time and show it only by a rounded or mis-shapen top or a dead apex. In north Scotland they escape bad thunderstorms and many have neat conic long spires now 45–50m tall. Within some 70 years of the first plantings, such is the rate of growth that a Giant sequoia was the biggest tree, over all, in every county. Now almost all these older trees have boles 2.0–2.8m in diameter.

The foliage is in hard, cord-like bunches with small scale leaves each with a protruding incurved point, variously deep green to blue-grey, on very stout shoots with long scales, yellowish or grey. When crushed the foliage has the scent of aniseed. Male flowers are very numerous at the tips of the minor shoots, pale yellow, shedding pollen unless frosted when they open, in February. The female flowers are quite large yellow and brown spiny globes 2cm across, solitary on stout stalks but bunched on short lengths of shoot. They ripen into woody cones 4–6cm long which remain on the tree for a few years. The seed is variably fertile from our trees depending on good weather in February, and better when imported from California but must be sown thinly. Trays or boxes of densely standing seedlings are liable to attack by grey mould (Botrytis cinerea). Young plants grow sturdy stems but not very fast in height and should be transplanted to beds in the first or second season, depending on size, and after 2 years there they should be 20–30cm and ready for planting out. Cuttings root well (some early avenues are cuttings from a single tree) and terminal shoots suitable are found curving to vertically upwards in large numbers on any tree with low branches.

Once established, the tree begins to grow more rapidly with each year for many years and after 10 years it should be about 7m × 15cm, but after thirty it can be 20m×70cm and a few are much more. They withstand a high degree of exposure unless on very thin soil over chalk and grow at a similar rate for a long time in almost any soil or region of Britain, but they are slow and thin in towns and not worth planting in cities.

The remarkably thick, fibrous and spongy bark is an adaptation to the natural fire-cycle of their native woods. Lightning causes the fires which tend to go through each area at about 15 year intervals. Much before that there is not enough fuel to sustain it but by then there is enough for a rapid burn which roasts the cones which are held with good seed for 20 years in California. The seed falls soon after, on the ash, and germinates together with seeds from the annual shedding of Douglas and White firs. When the next fire comes the sequoias are being suppressed by the firs which are taller, but the firs have thin, resinous bark which burns and they are killed, while the sequoia is protected by its thick bark.

SWAMP CYPRESS

Taxodium distichum

The Swamp cypress, known more as Baldcypress in America, grows by tidal creeks and inland river bottom-lands from Delaware round the coast to Texas and 1,100 miles up the Mississippi Valley. It was first grown here in 1640 and many were planted between 1750 and 1850 but it requires the long hot summers that all its native woods enjoy and so it thrives here only in East Anglia and the far south of England and is scarce and small further west and north. There are many fine trees around and in London and it is almost traditional to plant one beside a lake in any southern garden or park.

This tree is a redwood and is deciduous, like the Dawn redwood which it much resembles. The crown is less pointed and more irregular and twiggy than the Dawn redwood's and the much more slender leaves are spirally set not oppositely, on spirally arranged shoots. It leafs out very late, awaiting hot weather and is seldom green in general aspect until mid-June. It also colours late in the autumn, turning fox-red or orange-brown during late October and may hold its leaves, and the twigs that fall with them, until mid-December. It grows relatively slowly for a redwood, not often more than 50cm in a year and achieves 30m only in the best conditions. These are deep, rich, well-watered soils in some shelter, but it will grow perfectly well when far from water on most soils except very light sands.

The older trees bear bunches of male catkins, prominent through the winter and opening long and slender, in May. The same trees bear female flowers but some are likely to be more laden with one sex than the other. The cones are short-stalked, globular and pale green until ripening brown. The tree is raised from imported seed and yields narrow, upright well-shaped plants. Early planting out is safer but those going to a wet site can be planted late in spring even when 1.5–2.0m tall with success.

A feature of this tree is the woody 'knees', (pneumatophores) which are more like termite hills, smooth with brown bark and curved over at the rim of a sunken centre. Some impressive growths of these can be seen in some lakeside or riverside plantings but they arise only in such soils, or in boggy, winter-flooded hollows. They are not known around trees less than 40-years-old. They presumably aid the aeration of the roots which are in saturated soil, since they are made of a spongy tissue.

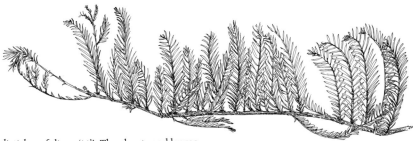

FIGURE 70
Swamp cypress *Taxodium distichum* foliage ($\times\frac{1}{2}$). The shoots and leaves, alternately set, both fall in late autumn.

Taxus baccata

The yew is native to Britain, northwards to Argyll and Perthshire and is very commonly planted in gardens, parks and churchyards. In a formal garden, yew is the best tree to form the hedges behind herbaceous borders, framing statuary, surrounding water-gardens and enclosed areas and making small vistas and barriers. It grows on any well-drained soil, can be clipped for hundreds of years, cut severely back, and withstand any weather for a thousand years. It is, in fact, by a very large factor, the longest living tree in northern Europe at least. Recent remeasurement of some churchyard yews show that growth in diameter is extraordinarily slow, sometimes 1cm in 20 years even in trees less than 2m through. Since many are 2.5–3.0m through they must be several thousand years old. The timber is exceptionally strong and durable and this enables trees to hold together when the boles are exceedingly hollow and other species would collapse from the weight of the branches. All the big yews have extensively hollow boles, often with aerial roots running down in the rotting wood and collected leaves to the ground. Old trees in churchyards are often only 10–12m tall, but some are 20m and in sheltered woods trees may exceed 25m.

FIGURE 71
First year yew seedling *Taxus baccata* (×1). Two seed-leaves appear, then normal foliage.

FIGURE 72
Spray of yew foliage bearing berries, autumn (×¾).

Yews are a very primitive form of conifer and instead of cones they bear succulent fruit that resemble berries. The males and females are on separate trees (another primitive feature in conifers). The males are little globes strung along the underside of the previous year's shoots and turn pale, almost white yellowish when shedding pollen in February. The females are sharply conic buds opening green and then resemble minute acorns in their cups. From the base of the 'acorn', a fleshy aril grows up almost to enfold the now black seed and this succulent flesh becomes bright red and sweet. The seed is, like every other part of the tree except the aril, highly poisonous to man and cattle, but not to deer or rabbits.

Wild groves of yew grow on open chalk downland but on clay soils they are under oak and on light soils they grow under beech. The yew can withstand a deeper shade than any other tree but then grows a rather thin, open crown and flowering is sparse or absent. The wood turns well and takes a fine polish, and is used for small parts of furniture and for turnery. It is a rich pinkish brown with prominent dark grain.

There are a great many cultivars of yew, differing from the wild tree in the habit and the arrangement and colour of foliage. The two most striking are:

'Dovastoniana'

West Felton yew. A tree planted in Shropshire in 1777 and now with a bole 107cm through, is the parent of those found in some gardens and parks with a straight central stem bearing long, level branches with hanging curtains of side-shoots and gently arched tips.

'Fastigiata'

Irish yew. Found on a hillside in county Fermanagh in about 1780, this dark, very upright yew is in almost every churchyard in the land. It is female and its long leaves spread in spirals from vertical shoots. It makes a broad, rounded old tree in eastern areas, and a tall, narrow tree to 16m in the west.

FIGURE 73
Irish yew *Taxus baccata* 'Fastigiata'. Sprig from the original tree in County Fermanagh, now about 220 years old (×⅔).

FIGURE 74
Silhouette of Irish yew, a tree common in churchyards.

WESTERN RED CEDAR

Thuja plicata

One of several species which are called 'cedar' but which are really in the Cypress family, this *Thuja* is abundant in gardens and parks everywhere, in shelterbelts and as a hedge and often as a huge specimen tree. It is also occasionally in plantations often underplanted in old larch crops, as it bears shade well and yields strong, light timber. This has specialist uses for ladder-poles and rugby goal posts, as well as commonly in timber-clad houses. The tree really thrives only in the western areas with humid air and high rainfall where it rapidly give a large volume of timber. It grows in the drier east quite adequately if planted on damp soil and it grows well on clay. In western gardens especially, heavy low branches will root if allowed to and form a thicket of trees around the parent stem, hiding and spoiling it. The natural range is from Alaska to California inland to Montana and the first seed was sent in 1853. The best trees are now over 40m tall and 1.5m diameter of bole.

FIGURE 75
One-year-old seedling of Western red cedar *Thuja plicata* showing solitary juvenile needles on upright main shoot, winter (×$\frac{1}{2}$).

FIGURE 76
Transplant of Western red cedar aged 3 years (2+1); only adult fern-like foliage is now seen, winter (×$\frac{1}{8}$).

The scale leaves are very small and clothe the shoots entirely. They are bright, often shining yellowish to mid-green above, have two pale streaks beneath and readily emit a strong aroma of pear-drops or pineapple which pervades the air near the trees on a warm calm day. The bark is dark brown and stringy and the crown is a variably slender conic shape but old trees may be irregular with big low branches. The tip of the tree is erect and in this it differs from the Lawson cypress (see page 20) which is, to a beginner a similar tree. The top of the Lawson droops in a pro-nounced arch, the tree also has a narrower, more pendulous crown and duller, harder foliage with a different scent.

The male flowers are very small, yellow globules on the tips of the shoots of mature trees and shed pollen in early March. The cones are leathery, flask-shaped with few but long scales and ripen brown. The very small seeds germinate with only two coty-ledons, then bear solitary needles spreading from the shoot. Only by the second year is the typical scaly foliage grown, and only then can they be identified.

A form with the foliage broadly but variably banded with bright yellow, 'Zebrina' arose in about 1900 and is very commonly planted in gardens. It makes a neat broad-conic tree and is one of the biggest growing golden conifers, some being already over 25m tall.

FIGURE 77
Foliage spray of Western red cedar showing slender cones fully opened, autumn (×⅓).

Tsuga heterophylla

This beautiful evergreen conifer owes its curious name to a supposed resemblance between the earthy smell of its crushed foliage and that of the hemlock plant, a tall, white-flowered poisonous perennial that grows beside rivers in southern England. Hemlock trees, however, come from North America and Asia, where several species are found, and this one grows along America's west coast, from Alaska to California. It is now being extensively planted in Britain because it starts growth well in the light shade of other trees, and eventually yields a very heavy timber crop.

Among commonly planted conifers, Western hemlock is recognised by an odd feature of its foliage; needles of various lengths are crowded together along the twigs in a random fashion. The seedling has three seed-leaves, an unusual number (see Figure 78). It needs shading in the seedbed. Transplants grow

FIGURE 78
Emergent seedling of Western hemlock *Tsuga heterophylla* with three seed-leaves (×1).

FIGURE 79
(right): One-year-old seedling of Western hemlock. The three seed-leaves are followed by typical needles of uneven lengths, winter (×$\frac{1}{2}$).

FIGURE 80
Three-year-old transplant of Western hemlock (2+1). The oblique growth is typical, and the leading shoot may even droop; but the trunk always grows upright, winter (×$\frac{1}{6}$).

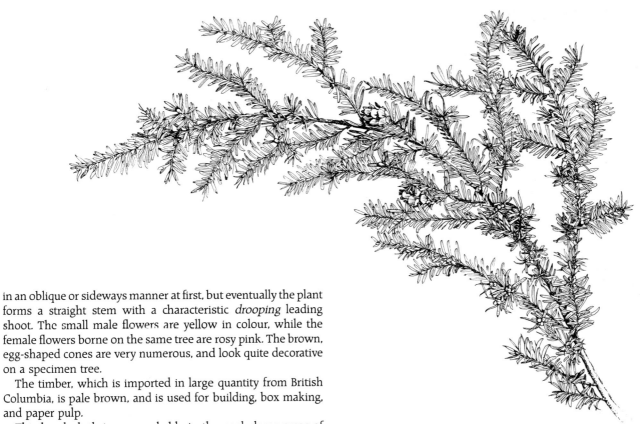

in an oblique or sideways manner at first, but eventually the plant forms a straight stem with a characteristic *drooping* leading shoot. The small male flowers are yellow in colour, while the female flowers borne on the same tree are rosy pink. The brown, egg-shaped cones are very numerous, and look quite decorative on a specimen tree.

The timber, which is imported in large quantity from British Columbia, is pale brown, and is used for building, box making, and paper pulp.

This hemlock thrives remarkably in the cool, damp areas of Scotland but in eastern England it needs moist sheltered sites or it becomes thin and unhealthy. In Scotland, many still growing very fast are 40–45m tall. Given plenty of moisture it grows equally well on clay or poor sands and quite well on peat, but not on chalky soil.

FIGURE 81
Foliage spray and cones of Western hemlock, autumn ($\times\frac{1}{3}$).

Conifer seeds

As shown in the drawings opposite, the seeds of conifers show remarkable variations in size and form, which are of considerable scientific interest and may help people to tell the different kinds apart. Seeds are fairly easily obtained by shaking newly ripened cones, or by cutting such cones through the centre, lengthwise, with a stout penknife.

In most species the seeds are borne two per scale, though not every scale carries well-filled and useful seeds. Most kinds bear wings, which are always removed by the forester later on, for convenience when storing or sowing seed. Our drawings, reproduced at about twice natural size, show the seeds from various aspects. In the pines, for example, the front view of the seed – plus its wing – differs from the back view. In the cone, the seed always lies towards the central axis, with the wing outside it, immediately against the scale. Pines have rather slender wings, which hold the oval seed in a little 'claw', made of two slender prongs. Scots pine has seeds of intermediate size, Corsican pine larger ones, and Lodgepole pine very small ones. Larches have rather triangular wings and also triangular seeds which are very firmly fixed to one side of the wing, less firmly on the other. Japanese larch seeds and wings are distinctly larger than those of the European kind.

In the spruces, the seed sits in a little cup at the base of the wing and is lightly attached on one side only; Sitka spruce seeds are exceptionally small. In Douglas fir, the seed is firmly fixed to one side of the wing and lightly to the other, but the oval shape prevents any confusion with the larches. The Noble fir and the Grand fir are easily known by the large size and wedge shape of both wing and seed, the two parts being firmly fixed together on both sides. Western hemlock is also fixed on both sides, but the seed is very small and the wing is oval.

In Western red cedar we find quite another pattern; there are two wings, extending equally on both sides of the seed, each about the same width as the seed itself. Lawson cypress bears similar seeds. Yew seeds are wingless, and oval in outline; they are borne within a pink fleshy cup, shown below the seed; there is only one seed in each berry. The juniper berries, drawn from three aspects, hold several small, hard, wingless, triangular seeds, which are also illustrated.

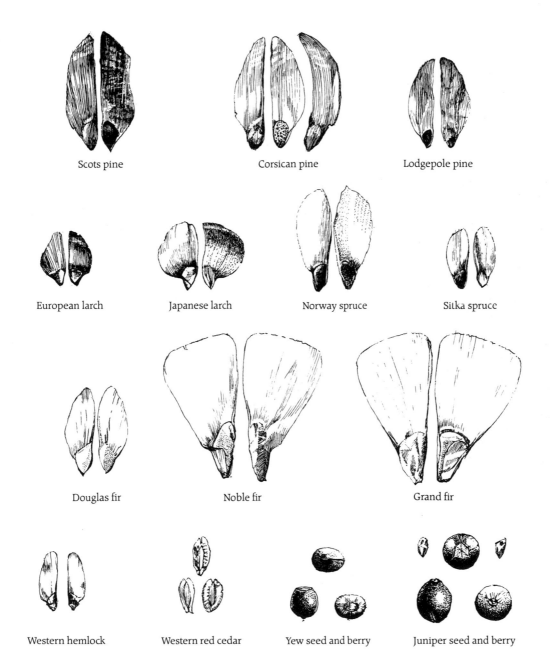

Scots pine

Corsican pine

Lodgepole pine

European larch

Japanese larch

Norway spruce

Sitka spruce

Douglas fir

Noble fir

Grand fir

Western hemlock

Western red cedar

Yew seed and berry

Juniper seed and berry

Index

Printed in the UK for HMSO
Dd 736984   C150   5/85